T. Rex to Go

T. Rex to Go

Build Your Own from
Chicken Bones

CHRIS McGOWAN

HarperPerennial

A Division of HarperCollinsPublishers

HarperCollins books may be purchased for educational, business, or sales promotional use. For information please write: Special Markets Department, HarperCollins Publishers, Inc., 10 East 53rd Street, New York, NY 10022.

FIRST EDITION

Designed by Helene Wald Berinsky

Library of Congress Cataloging-in-Publication Data
McGowan, Christopher.
T-rex to go : build your own from chicken bones / Chris McGowan. — 1st ed.
p.   cm.
ISBN 0–06–095281–4
1. Tyrannosaurus rex—Models.   2. Models and model making.
I. Title
QE862.S3M334   1999
567.912'9'0228—dc21   98-37526

---

99 00 01 02 03 ❖/RRD 10 9 8 7 6 5 4 3 2 1

To the *T. rex* builders:

Judith, A.J., Allison, Caitlin, Chase, Chelsi, Colby,

Geoffrey, Josh, Katie, Lisa, Nick, and Randi

Contents

Preface

The popularity of dinosaurs never fails to amaze me. The appeal is not confined to youngsters, either. When we have our open house at Toronto's Royal Ontario Museum, there are just as many parents who want to chat about dinosaurs as there are small children. I should therefore not have been surprised at the response to my first book on dinosaur building, *Make Your Own Dinosaur out of Chicken Bones*. I got letters and phone calls and E-mails from all over the world. More gratifying still were the photos I received from people who had built their own miniature *Apatosaurus* skeletons. The model builders ranged in age from twelve-year-old A.J., from Massachusetts, who built a dinosaur named Harold, to adults, like Colby Kavanagh, who displayed "Veronica" in her Arizona bookstore. There was one enthusiastic group of teenagers at a school in Colorado who had built a whole herd of *Apatosaurus*! Keen to try another dinosaur, I sent them the first draft of the present book. The result was a *Tyrannosaurus* herd, lots of valuable feedback, and some great ideas. They had many adventures, and misadventures, along the way. I shall share some of these, and their ideas, in the second part of the book. My sincere thanks to the entire class: Geoffrey, Nick, Luke, Katie, Chase, Lisa, Mathew, Chelsi, Randi, Josh, Daniel, Allison, Nick, and Caitlin, and to their teacher, Judith Miller Smith. I also wish to thank my paleontological colleague, Kevin

Padian, for reading parts of the manuscript and giving me so much valuable feedback. Thanks also to John Attridge, my old Ph.D. supervisor, and to Larry Martin, for valuable discussions on their views of bird/dinosaur relationships. My good friend Sheila Sherwood carefully and patiently proofread the copyedited manuscript with me, for which I thank her warmly.

Working with the professionals at HarperCollins has been the same joy as before. I thank them for their corporate enthusiasm for the project, and for their sense of good fun. Particular thanks to my editor, Trena Keating, for her editorial and logistic help, her encouragement, and for acting *in loco parentis* during Norman's trips to New York. My thanks also to Bronson Elliott for her editorial assistance and for always being at the other end of the phone; to Dan Cuddy for his careful production editing; to Helene Wald Berinsky, who designed the book; and to Doreen Louie, who designed the jacket.

Jill Grinberg, the best agent anyone could ever wish for, enthusiastically championed the project from the outset, giving support and encouragement and solid practical advice, for which I am truly grateful. Participating with Julian Mulock in another joint venture has been both rewarding and enjoyable, as always. Not only did he draw all the fine illustrations, but his building of a model *T. rex* provided valuable insights that have been incorporated.

Last, but certainly not least, I acknowledge the enthusiastic interest and support of the single most important part of my life, my family—Liz, Claire, Angela, Rob, and Sloan.

Part I

▼▼▼▼▼▼▼▼▼▼▼

Are Birds Feathered Dinosaurs?

Every year a gathering of people professionally interested in prehistoric animals meets in a city somewhere in North America. The 1996 annual meeting of the Society of Vertebrate Paleontology (SVP) was held in the American Museum of Natural History (AMNH), in New York, that great bastion of things dinosaurian. This was déjà vu for me, because the first SVP meeting I ever attended was held at the AMNH, way back in 1969. What a lot has changed in those intervening years. At the 1969 meeting there were only about half the number of people as those attending the 1996 meeting. This was long before the time of dinosaur mania (probably started by the new ideas and new finds of the seventies), and there were precious few presentations on dinosaurs. Today, the number of dinosaur researchers is so large that a whole day is set aside for their presentations. New dinosaur discoveries are being made at such a pace that it is difficult to keep current. These are interesting times to be a paleontologist.

Among the relatively few people interested in dinosaurs during the sixties, it was considered that dinosaurs became extinct at the end of the Cretaceous period—about 65 million years ago—without leaving descendants. Paleontologists were certainly aware of the old idea that birds evolved from dinosaurs, a notion

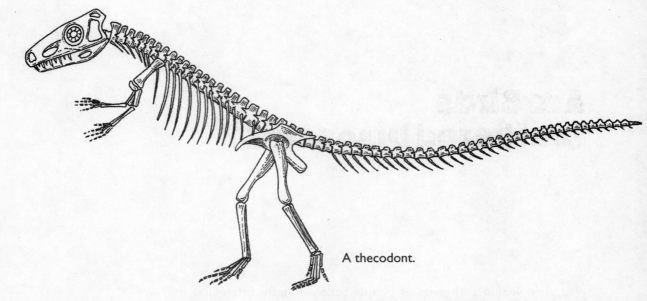

A thecodont.

dating back to Darwin's time, but that notion was no longer accepted. Instead, most paleontologists thought that birds had evolved from a group of more primitive reptiles, called the thecodonts.* According to this scheme of things both birds and dinosaurs evolved, independently, from thecodonts.

Dinosaurs are a diverse group of land animals that includes meat-eaters, like the giant *Tyrannosaurus* and the chicken-sized *Compsognathus,* and an array of plant-eaters, like *Triceratops, Stegosaurus, Euoplocephalus, Corythosaurus,* and *Diplodocus.* The group to which *Tyrannosaurus* and *Compsognathus* belong is called the **theropods**.

The originator of the idea that birds evolved from dinosaurs, specifically from theropod dinosaurs, was Thomas Henry Huxley (1825–1895). He reached this conclusion after comparing *Megalosaurus,* the first dinosaur to be named (it was a meat-eater, like *Tyrannosaurus*) and the ostrich. Huxley also made a careful study of *Archaeopteryx,* the oldest known bird. The first skeleton of *Archaeopteryx* was discovered in 1861, just two years after the

*For technical reasons to do with classification procedures, the term *thecodont* is no longer widely used.

Diplodocus, Tyrannosaurus, Stegosaurus, Euoplocephalus, Corythosaurus, Compsognathus, and *Triceratops.* All drawn to the same scale, so the smallest ones look really small.

publication of Charles Darwin's revolutionary book *The Origin of Species.* The timing of the find could hardly have been more appropriate, because this chicken-sized animal was a reptile in all its skeletal features (save one, the wishbone, which will be discussed later), but it had wings and feathers. Here, then, was a fossil that bridged the gap between two major groups, the birds and the reptiles, providing tangible evidence for evolution.

Archaeopteryx has all the skeletal features of a small theropod dinosaur. It has often been said that if it had not been for the feather impressions, preserved in the fine-grained limestone in which the skeleton was found, it would have been identified as a small dinosaur. Indeed, two of the seven skeletons of *Archaeopteryx* that have now been collected were initially identified as *Compsognathus,* because their faint feather impressions had been overlooked.

The wing feathers of *Archaeopteryx* are just like those of a modern bird. There is a central mid-rib, called the **rachis**, which is offset toward the front, or leading edge, of the feather. There are aerodynamic reasons for this asymmetry, which is said to relate to the way the individual feathers twist during the wing

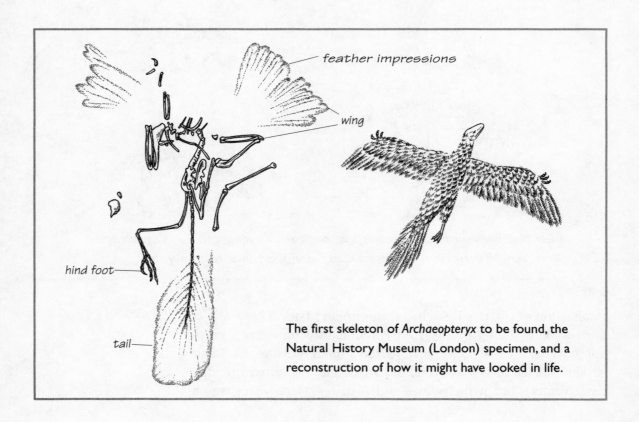

feather impressions

wing

hind foot

tail

The first skeleton of *Archaeopteryx* to be found, the Natural History Museum (London) specimen, and a reconstruction of how it might have looked in life.

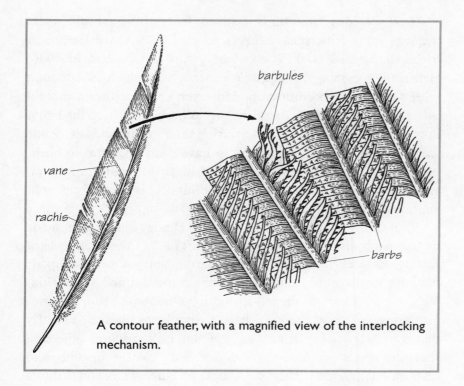

A contour feather, with a magnified view of the interlocking mechanism.

beat cycle. During the downbeat, which is the power stroke, the twisting of the feathers causes them to press tightly together, forming an airtight seal. The reverse happens during the upbeat, which is a recovery stroke, allowing air to pass between the feathers, thereby reducing the wind resistance.

The rachis gives off numerous branches, called **barbs**. The barbs, in turn, give off even smaller branches, called **barbules**. These minute structures hook onto adjacent barbules, like velcro, thereby maintaining the integrity of the whole unit, called the **vane**. This type of feather, which is stiff, is called a **contour feather**. Other feathers lack a rachis and interlocking barbules, and are therefore soft and fluffy, like the down feathers.

Besides feathers, the only other avian feature of *Archaeopteryx* is the wishbone, or **furcula**. This bone represents the fused collarbones, or **clavicles**. The furcula of *Archaeopteryx* looks like a boomerang.

Furcula of *Archaeopteryx*.

Huxley's idea that birds evolved from theropod dinosaurs received some criticisms, and was rejected by Gerhard Heilmann in his influential book *The Origin of Birds*, published in 1926. Heilmann recognized that *Archaeopteryx* had much in common with small theropod dinosaurs. However, since neither a furcula nor clavicles had been found in any dinosaur, he reasoned that they must have lost these bones during their evolution. Theropods were accordingly too specialized to have been ancestral to birds. Heilmann therefore sought a more primitive ancestor, and concluded that birds evolved from thecodonts. This became the conventional wisdom that persisted into the late sixties.

John Ostrom, of Yale University, like Huxley before him, made an extensive study of *Archaeopteryx,* but he had the advantage of having more skeletons to examine. Also, many more theropods have been discovered and old skeletons reexamined since Huxley's time. Some of these—including *Oviraptor, Albertosaurus, Daspletosaurus,* and *Ingenia*—have a furcula, as does the recently discovered *Scipionyx* from Italy. Heilmann's original objection that theropods were too specialized was clearly invalid, and Ostrom championed the resurrection of Huxley's original thesis that birds are the direct descendants of dinosaurs. Although there have been some dissenters, Ostrom's ideas, which appeared during the 1970s, are widely accepted among paleontologists.

With the advent of **cladistics**, the relationships between birds and dinosaurs have been demonstrated even further. Cladistics is the classification system whereby branched groups (often of species), or **clades**, are established based on the sharing of new evolutionary features, called **derived characters**. The species represented by the branches of the clade are said to share a **common ancestor**, and are described as being **monophyletic**. A monophyletic group contains all the descendants of the common ancestor. Two branches sharing a common ancestor are said to be **sister groups**. For example, cats—including lions, ocelots, tigers, domestic cats, and cheetahs—belong to one monophyletic group. All cats are united by a number of shared derived characters, which includes the ability to retract their claws and the effective loss of all teeth behind the slicing cheek teeth (called carnassials).

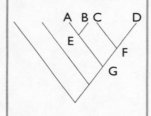

A cladogram. A and B are sister groups, sharing a common ancestor, E. Similarly, C and D are sister groups, sharing a common ancestor, F. E and F are also sister groups, sharing a common ancestor, G.

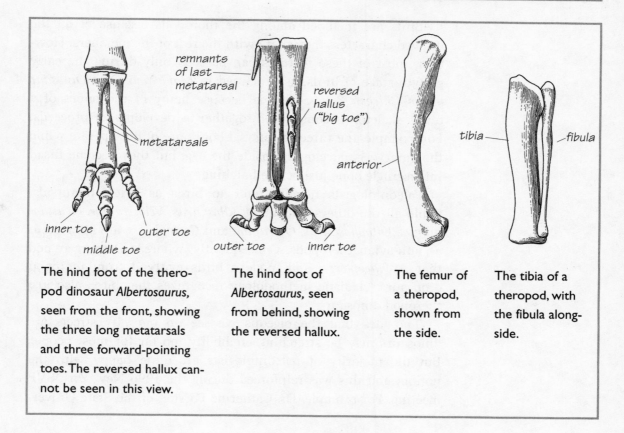

remnants
of last
metatarsal

reversed
hallus
("big toe")

metatarsals

anterior

tibia

fibula

inner toe

outer toe

middle toe

outer toe

inner toe

The hind foot of the theropod dinosaur *Albertosaurus*,
seen from the front, showing
the three long metatarsals
and three forward-pointing
toes. The reversed hallux cannot be seen in this view.

The hind foot of
Albertosaurus, seen
from behind, showing
the reversed hallux.

The femur of
a theropod,
shown from
the side.

The tibia of a
theropod, with
the fibula along-
side.

Similarly, *Archaeopteryx* shares a suite of derived characters with
dinosaurs like *Tyrannosaurus* and *Compsognathus*. They form a
monophyletic group, the theropods. These features include: a foot
supported by three long **metatarsal** bones (these are tightly
pressed together and are often fused, that is, joined); three main
toes and a short "big toe," all ending in claws; a "big toe," called
the **reversed hallux**, that faces backward; a **femur** (thighbone)
that is slightly bowed forward; a **fibula** (the thin bone that runs
along the outside of the shinbone) that is closely pressed against
the **tibia** (shinbone); an extension from one of the ankle bones
that overlaps the lower end of the tibia, called the **ascending
process of the astragalus**; and a hand with three fingers, each
ending in a sharp claw.

Birds are included among the theropods because of all the derived characters they share with the rest of the members. However, most of these features can be seen only during the early growth stage of birds, as explained in *Make Your Own Dinosaur out of Chicken Bones*. This is because many of the bones of a bird's skeleton become fused together as development proceeds. For example, the three metatarsal bones are quite separate while the embryo is developing inside the egg, but they become fused into a single bone just before hatching.

Paleontologists usually refer to birds as avian theropods, while all the others, including *Allosaurus, Velociraptor, Ornithomimus, Dilophosaurus, Oviraptor,* and *Coelophysis,* are referred to as non-avian theropods. Consequently, whereas Ostrom argued that *Archaeopteryx* and modern birds **evolved** from theropod dinosaurs, cladistic methodology recognizes that birds also **are** theropod dinosaurs.

The idea that the pigeons we see on our city streets are dinosaurs may be stretching credibility too far for most people. But the majority of paleontologists are quite happy with the notion, and this was reinforced during the 1996 New York SVP meeting. For example, Dr. Catherine Forster, of the State Univer-

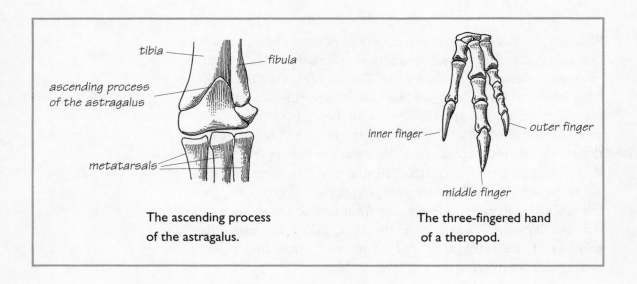

tibia

fibula

ascending process
of the astragalus

metatarsals

The ascending process
of the astragalus.

inner finger

outer finger

middle finger

The three-fingered hand
of a theropod.

Dinosaurs, Hips, and Classification

Theropods, like their sister group, the plant-eating sauropods, to which *Apatosaurus* belongs, have a three-pronged pelvis, comprising the **ilium** (above), the **pubis** (in front), and the **ischium** (behind). Many theropods have a long ilium that extends well forward of the hip socket. Sauropods, in contrast, have a much shorter and broader ilium. Dinosaurs with a three-pronged pelvis are collectively referred to as the Saurischia.

All other dinosaurs have a four-pronged pelvis, because the pubis has two prongs, and are collectively called the Ornithischia. Ornithischian dinosaurs include the hadrosaurs, stegosaurs, horned dinosaurs, and ankylosaurs.

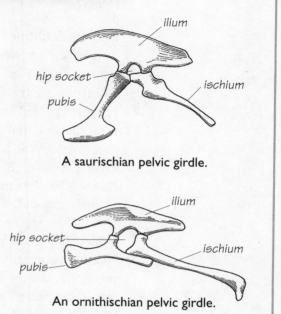

A saurischian pelvic girdle.

An ornithischian pelvic girdle.

sity of New York, gave an account of a recently discovered bird skeleton from the Cretaceous Period that was found in Madagascar. What was so remarkable about this bird was that its foot had a large retractable claw, just like that of *Velociraptor* and its relatives—collectively called **dromaeosaurs**. And then there was the Chinese delegate who was showing photographs, outside the meeting rooms, of the new dinosaur *Sinosauropteryx,* from China. What caught everyone's attention about *Sinosauropteryx* was that it had what appeared to be a series of wispy featherlike structures running along its neck and back. The whole meeting was soon buzzing with the news that the first feathered dinosaur had been discovered. One of the color slides that Catherine Forster showed in her presentation was a cartoon of a feathered creature lying on a psychiatrist's couch. "Am I a bird or a dinosaur?" asked the bewildered misfit. This summed up the situation very well because it seemed that the dividing line between birds and dinosaurs had disappeared. Few delegates, I suspect, left that meeting doubting that birds really were just feathered dinosaurs.

Then there was the Chicago meeting in 1997. I knew things were going to be different because I had received a telephone call from my friend John Ruben, a physiologist, several months earlier. He told me of the startling findings from his laboratory that showed that birds could not possibly be closely related to dinosaurs. As it happened, John's call came the day before I left on a trip to publicize *Make Your Own Dinosaur out of Chicken Bones*. This was the book in which I said that birds *are* dinosaurs, so his news did not come at exactly the right moment! Physiologists are concerned with the inner workings of living things, and Ruben has made some major contributions to our knowledge of reptiles, especially regarding their activity levels. I have an enormous respect for his work, so he had my full attention. He told me of the recent discoveries he had made with his collaborators. Their evidence, based on the differences between the lungs of reptiles and birds, supported the view that theropods and birds were unrelated, and that the former could not possibly have given rise to the latter. Before looking at their evidence, I need to say something about the lungs of mammals, reptiles, and birds.

Our body cavity, like that of all other mammals, is divided into two parts by the **diaphragm**. This muscular partition stretches across the body at the base of the rib cage, forming an airtight seal between the **thoracic cavity**, housing the lungs and heart, and the **abdominal cavity** beneath it. The abdominal cavity houses the gut, liver, and other abdominal organs. The lungs are ventilated by the combined action of the diaphragm and rib cage. During inspiration the dome-shaped diaphragm is pulled down and the ribs are raised, both actions increasing the volume of the thoracic cavity, thereby reducing the internal pressure. The reverse happens on expiration, increasing the thoracic pressure, thereby forcing air out of the lungs. Mammals, being active animals with high **metabolic rates** (the rate at which oxygen is used by the body), require efficient lungs. The lungs have to rapidly absorb oxygen from the inspired air, and get rid of the carbon dioxide accumulated in the blood. This **gaseous exchange** can only take place at the moist internal surface of the lungs. If the lungs were simple sacs, like balloons, the total surface area of their lining would be too small for the high rate of gaseous exchange demanded of the high metabolic rate. To this end the lungs are subdivided into millions of small sacs, called **alveoli**, whose combined surface area is enormous. Therefore,

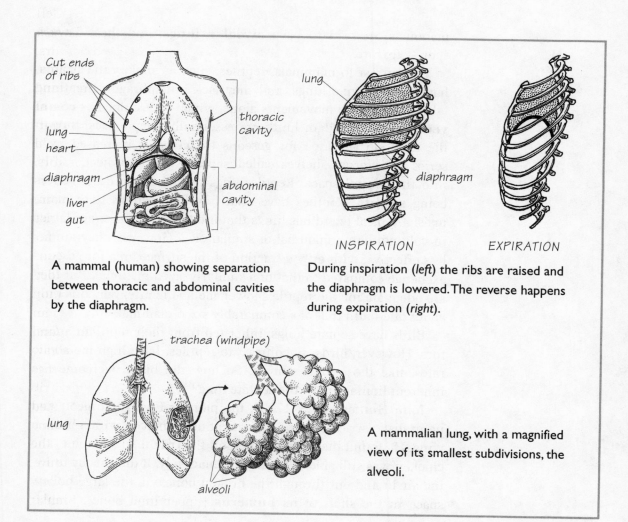

Cut ends of ribs

lung

thoracic cavity

lung

heart

diaphragm

liver

gut

abdominal cavity

A mammal (human) showing separation between thoracic and abdominal cavities by the diaphragm.

lung

diaphragm

INSPIRATION

EXPIRATION

During inspiration (*left*) the ribs are raised and the diaphragm is lowered. The reverse happens during expiration (*right*).

trachea (windpipe)

lung

alveoli

A mammalian lung, with a magnified view of its smallest subdivisions, the alveoli.

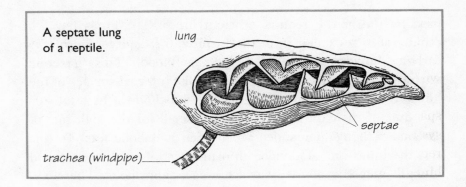

A septate lung of a reptile.

mammals are said to have **alveolar lungs**, and these have a spongy texture.

In contrast to mammals, reptiles, such as snakes and lizards, have fairly simple lungs, and they lack a diaphragm. Breathing takes place by rib movements alone, which is described as **costal ventilation**. Reptilian lungs are essentially simple sacs, though the total surface area for gaseous exchange is increased by a series of internal shelves called **septae**, which project, stiffly, into the central space. Reptile lungs are therefore described as being **septate**. Reptiles have relatively larger lungs than mammals: a typical lizard has lungs that are two to seven times larger in volume than a mammal of similar size. However, they are far less effective, with only a fraction of the surface area for gaseous exchange compared to that of a similarly sized mammal. But they are adequate for the reptile's lower metabolic rate, which is only about one-tenth that of a comparably sized mammal.

Birds have septate lungs, inherited from their reptilian ancestors. However, birds, in contrast to reptiles, have high metabolic rates, like those of mammals. So how did birds overcome the inherent limitations of the septate lung?

John Hunter (1728–1793), the pioneer English surgeon and naturalist, carried out an experiment on a chicken with a broken wing. He found that when he tied off the **trachea** (windpipe) the chicken was still able to breathe. Remarkably, it did this by drawing air in and out through the broken bone, via the large hollow space in the shaft of its **humerus** (upper limb bone). Similar results were obtained for a hawk with a broken leg, where the bird breathed through its femur. These experiments showed that the hollow spaces inside a bird's bones are somehow connected with its lungs, which is most bizarre.

Not only do a bird's lungs communicate with the hollow spaces of its bones, but they are also connected with an extensive system of thin-walled and inflatable sacs called **air sacs**. Like all reptiles, except crocodiles (the closest living reptile to birds), birds lack a diaphragm. However, they have a unique and efficient system of costal ventilation involving a modification of the rib cage. In addition to the regular ribs, which articulate with the **vertebral column** (backbone), there is a second set, and these

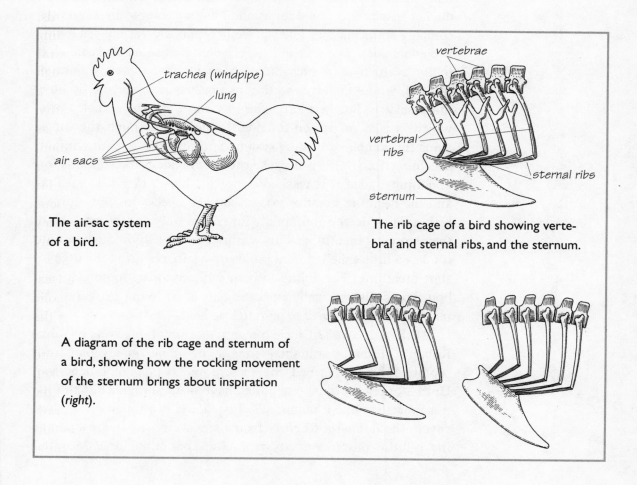

The air-sac system of a bird.

The rib cage of a bird showing vertebral and sternal ribs, and the sternum.

A diagram of the rib cage and sternum of a bird, showing how the rocking movement of the sternum brings about inspiration (*right*).

articulate with the **sternum** (breastbone). These two sets of ribs are referred to as **vertebral ribs** and **sternal ribs** respectively. Ventilation is brought about by the rocking movement of the sternum, which expands and contracts the rib cage, decreasing, then increasing the thoracic pressure. When the pressure inside the thoracic cavity is decreased the air sacs are inflated, the reverse happening when the pressure increases.

The air sacs have few blood vessels, and are not involved in gaseous exchange—their function is only to ventilate the lungs. Birds have relatively small lungs, and these are fairly rigid and do not expand and contract during breathing, in contrast to the lungs of mammals and reptiles. But their most remarkable feature is that the air flows in only one direction, and is continuous, both during inspiration and expiration. This is achieved by the fairly complex shunting that takes place between the various interconnected air sacs. The system is so efficient that some birds are able to fly as high as twenty-three thousand feet (seven thousand meters), where the air is so thin as to cause mammals to become unconscious. Furthermore, because some of the exhaled air, which is rich in carbon dioxide, is recycled through the lungs using the complex shunting system, birds are able to pant without becoming dizzy. This is because carbon dioxide is the stimulus for breathing, and if it is washed out of the blood, dizziness results, and the desire to breathe ceases. You can check this for yourself by breathing deeply and rapidly for fifteen to twenty seconds, and then stopping breathing. This washes out the carbon dioxide, and it takes a little time before it builds up again, restoring the urge to start breathing. The ability to pant without losing too much carbon dioxide is especially important to birds living in warm climates, where they need to pant to lose heat.

At the same 1997 Chicago meeting, Terry Jones, one of John Ruben's graduate students, after a preamble on alveolar and septate lungs, described the respiratory system of crocodiles. Unlike other reptiles, crocodiles have a diaphragm, but this is not muscular like a mammal's. Instead, it is a tough sheet that covers the domed **anterior** (front) surface of the liver, separating off the thoracic cavity from the abdominal one. Muscles

lung   liver   diaphragm muscles

pubis

Longitudinal section through a crocodile showing the hepatic-piston system.

attach to the liver from the pubis, and when these contract they pull the liver back, like a piston. When the muscles relax the liver springs back into its original position. This unique system, referred to as the **hepatic piston**, works in concert with the expansion and contraction of the rib cage to ventilate the lungs. The large, forwardly directed pubis is an integral part of the mechanism, providing a large attachment area for the muscles that drive the piston.

Jones then argued that theropods like *Allosaurus* have a pubis similar to that of their relatives the crocodiles, suggesting a similar hepatic-piston ventilation mechanism. Supporting evidence appeared to be provided by the photograph of the supposedly feathered dinosaur, *Sinosauropteryx*. The photograph showed a dark outline in the abdominal region, with a curved anterior edge at the level of the base of the rib cage, reminiscent of the curved anterior edge of the crocodilian hepatic piston. And the fact that theropods lack the sternal ribs and well-developed sternum of birds ruled out any possibility that they had an air-sac ventilation system.

One implication of theropods having had an hepatic-piston respiratory system is that they could not have been as active as birds and mammals, because of the limitations of gaseous exchange. But the most important implication is that birds, with their air-sac system of lung ventilation, could not possibly have evolved from an ancestor with an hepatic-piston system. This is because it would have involved an untenable transition from a system reliant on an airtight diaphragm to one in which there was no diaphragm at all.

The second presentation by the group was given by Nicholas Geist, another of John Ruben's graduate students. He argued that the external structures running along the neck and back of *Sinosauropteryx,* the supposedly feathered dinosaur from China, were not feathers at all, but merely fibers. Similar conclusions were reached by a small group of paleontologists—made up of both proponents and opponents of the bird–dinosaur connection—who had visited China to examine the specimens. My colleague Larry Martin, one of the opponents in the group, told me the decision was reached because nobody could see any feather structures, neither rachis nor barbs. He was convinced that the structures actually lay below the skin.

The third attack on the bird–dinosaur relationship came as a reminder. In a paper that appeared in the journal *Science* on the development of the hand, the authors, Ann Burke and Alan Feduccia, reiterated the work of others. There has been a long-standing controversy over the identity of the three separate fingers that appear during the early development of birds. Many **tetrapods** (four-limbed animals—amphibians, reptiles, birds, and mammals), ourselves included, have five fingers, while many others have undergone some losses. The question of interest here is which fingers were lost during the evolution of the birds from their five-fingered ancestor. Embryologists have generally held that birds have lost their thumb and small finger, based on their studies of which fingers fail to grow. Loss of the thumb and little finger commonly occurs during digital reduction, as in the rhinoceros, which also has only three fingers. Accordingly, the three fingers of a bird were identified as digits 2, 3, and 4.

Theropod dinosaurs typically have three fingers, though the earliest ones had more. Paleontologists have long held that the three fingers represent digits 1, 2, and 3, because digits 4 and 5 are already much reduced in five-fingered dinosaurs. For example, in *Herrerasaurus,* one of the earliest dinosaurs, which may be a theropod (there has been some debate), digit 5 has almost disappeared, and digit 4 is exceedingly short.

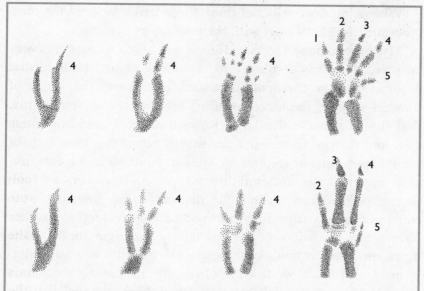

The development of the forelimb in the alligator (*top*) and chicken. Redrawn from Burke and Feduccia article cited in Further Reading appendix.

It is difficult to reconcile the evolution of the avian hand, which seemingly retains digits 2, 3, and 4, with a theropod ancestor that retains digits 1, 2, and 3. I, like most other paleontologists, have been aware of the problem for years, but chose to ignore it. The *Science* article, which introduced some additional embryological evidence supporting the 2, 3, 4 count for birds, served as a reminder, pointing out that the fourth digit predominates during early development. This is true for most living reptiles and mammals, both for the hand and the foot. Burke and Feduccia compared the developmental stages of the hand in an alligator, chicken, and turtle, identifying the predominant digit as the fourth in each case. The fifth digit was retained in the alligator and turtle, but appeared to have only a fleeting presence in the chicken, during a later stage of development. Their study seemed to leave no room for doubt that the bird's hand comprised digits 2, 3, and 4.

What should we make of these three strikes against the bird-dinosaur case? Let's start with the respiratory evidence.

My initial reaction to John Ruben and his colleagues was very positive. Here was a compelling argument against birds having descended from theropod dinosaurs. However, the longer I thought about it, the less compelling I found it. The first point is that the possession of a large, forward-directed pubis in crocodiles and theropods does not necessarily mean that they had the same hepatic-piston respiratory system. Sauropods, for example, also have a large, forward-directed pubis. However, as John Ruben pointed out during our discussion, an hepatic piston could not have worked in a sauropod because its large gut would have got in the way—herbivores have a large gut for the slow digestion of plant food. Lacking the sternal ribs and large sternum of birds, sauropods were obviously not air-sac ventilators either*. They were probably costal breathers, relying on their ribs for ventilation. If sauropods were costal breathers, why not theropods too?

A second point is that although it is tempting to interpret the outline of soft parts in the body cavity of *Sinosauropteryx* as evidence of an hepatic piston, this is very circumstantial. This is because the preservation of the soft anatomy in fossils can be very misleading, and is often subject to a wide range of interpretations. For example, there has been a considerable amount of controversy over the interpretation of the outlines of the wing membranes in pterosaurs. However, I must point out that John Ruben's presented some convincing evidence at the 1998 SVP meeting in Snowbird, Utah, to show that the small theropod dinosaur *Scipionyx* had an hepatic-piston respiratory system.

A third, less significant point is that not all theropods had a forward-directed pubis. In the dromaeosaurs, for example, the theropod group that includes *Velociraptor* and *Deinonychus*, the pubis is directed backward.

---

*The hollow excavations called **pleurocoels** in the sides of many sauropod vertebrae have been interpreted as evidence for air sacs. However, they could simply be to reduce the weight of the skeleton.

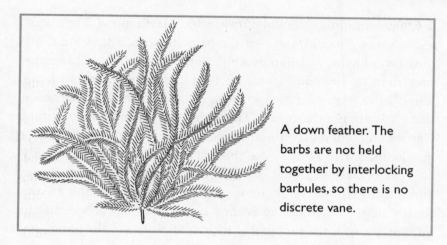

A down feather. The barbs are not held together by interlocking barbules, so there is no discrete vane.

The finding that the structures projecting from the body of *Sinosauropteryx* lack a rachis and barbs, features that maintain the integrity of the vane, is not a serious problem. Feathers come in a wide variety of forms in modern birds, including the fluffy down feathers that lack a vane and serve an insulatory role. Even if the structures have nothing to do with a body covering—they could be an artifact of preservation—this would not be evidence against a bird–dinosaur relationship, any more than the absence of fur from mammal-like reptile fossils (synapsids) could be taken as evidence that they were not ancestral to mammals.

The discrepancy between the fingers of modern birds and theropod dinosaurs appears to be an insurmountable problem, but there is a solution. Early dinosaurs (from the late Triassic period) are quite rare, but we have good information for a few of them, including the theropod *Coelophysis*. *Coelophysis* has lost digit 5 and has a much reduced fourth finger, which is entirely lost in later theropods. As pointed out by Feduccia, a staunch opponent of the idea that birds evolved from dinosaurs, the usual digits to be lost in tetrapods are digits 1 and 5. The retention of digit 1 in theropods, and the loss of digit 4, the predominant digit, is therefore most unusual. Thus, although the fourth digit pre-dominates during hand development in most tetrapods, this is not true for theropods. So if we could study the early embryonic development of the hand of a three-fingered theropod, like *Compsognathus,* we would find that the principal finger was the third, the fourth having failed to develop. Burke and Feduccia's assumption that the predominant finger in the developing chicken's hand is the fourth digit, as in most other tetrapods, presupposed that birds are not theropods. This point was made by their critics, Garner and Thomas, who argue that the predominant digit in a developing bird's hand is the third. The small finger that briefly appears behind this digit, identified as the fifth digit by Burke and Feduccia, would therefore represent the remains of the fourth digit. This line of reasoning makes perfectly good sense to me, and resolves the problem of incompatibilities in the hand.

Archaeopteryx is recognized as a bird by both sides in the debate. Proponents view all the derived features it shares with theropod dinosaurs, such as *Compsognathus,* as evidence for their close relationship. However, opponents view these characters as being **convergent**, meaning that they evolved in two distantly related groups simply because the animals adapted to the same environment. An example of convergence is the similarity in body shape between dolphins and sharks. Both groups have streamlined bodies because both swim rapidly in the sea, but their similar shape has nothing to do with relationships, and they are only very distantly related. I find it hard to accept that all the skeletal similarities between *Archaeopteryx* and theropod dinosaurs are due to convergence, especially since one is a flier and the others are not.

Another argument of the opponents of the bird–dinosaur relationship is that some of the characters uniting *Archaeopteryx* and theropods are not exactly the same in each case. Characters that are exactly the same are said to be **homologous**, so their argument is that the characters are not homologous. Feduccia, in his fine book *The Origin and Evolution of Birds,* systematically goes through a large number of derived characters that birds and theropod dinosaurs share, rejecting many of them as being non-homologous. For example, *Archaeopteryx,* like modern birds, has a reversed hallux ("big toe"). A similar feature is found in theropod dinosaurs, but Feduccia claims that the hallux never faces backward in dinosaurs, facing inward instead, so that the two features are not homologous. The Royal Ontario Museum's skeleton of *Albertosaurus,* close relative of *Tyrannosaurus,* has a backward-facing big toe, and is on display in the Dinosaur Gallery for all the world to see. The same is true for other theropods too.

The debate over the relationship between birds and dinosaurs, like other controversies in paleontology, can be resolved only by the discovery of new fossils. Such finds seem to be occurring at a phenomenal rate these days, and two new dinosaurs, *Protarchaeopteryx* and *Caudipteryx,* were reported in the media just as I was finishing writing this book. What made these particular discoveries so special, though, was that they were the first dinosaurs ever to be found that had true feathers. These small theropods—each less than a meter long—were from the same Chinese locality as *Sinosauropteryx*. There is some doubt over the exact age of this locality—it is either Late Jurassic or Early Cretaceous—making the skeletons between about 150 and 130 million years old. As such, they are either the same age as, or a little younger than, *Archaeopteryx*. There is a single specimen of *Protarchaeopteryx,* and two of *Caudipteryx,* but none is complete, so some questions remain regarding their structures. As in *Archaeopteryx,* each partial skeleton has the anatomy of a small theropod dinosaur, and it is only the presence of feather impressions that make them so remarkable. But in spite of their feathers, their relatively small forelimbs seem to rule out any possibility of flight. The forelimb in *Archaeopteryx* is about the same length as the hind limb, but it is only about two-thirds as long in *Protarchaeopteryx,* and only about half as long in *Caudipteryx.*

Feather impressions have only been preserved in parts of the specimens, including portions of the forelimb, tail, breast, and leg, but there are so many of them that we have a good idea of their structure. As in modern birds, there are down feathers, lacking a rachis and interlocking barbules, and contour feathers, with a rachis and a stiff vane. The integrity of the vane strongly suggests there was an interlocking mechanism between the barbules. All of the feathers appear to have a centrally placed rachis, making the vane symmetrical. The wing feathers of *Archaeopteryx* and other flying birds, in contrast, have asymmetrical vanes. The feathers appear to be relatively shorter than in *Archaeopteryx* too. Furthermore, the tail feathers appear to be restricted to the tip, rather than occurring along most of its length as in *Archaeopteryx*. These observations are further evidence that *Protarchaeopteryx* and *Caudipteryx* were nonfliers.

What should we make of these two new dinosaurian discoveries? Before attempting to answer this question I should emphasize that *Protarchaeopteryx* and *Caudipteryx* are both incompletely known, so the picture may change with new discoveries. Opponents of the idea that birds are theropods dismiss *Protarchaeopteryx* and *Caudipteryx* as birds that have lost the power of flight. Larry Martin holds this view. He made the point in a recent conversation that these animals have particularly large hands, a feature that is typically avian. *Archaeopteryx,* for example, has a hand that is much longer than its femur (1.5 times longer), and the same is true for *Protarchaeopteryx* (1.2 times longer). However, in *Caudipteryx* the hand is much shorter than the femur (0.6 times as long), shorter even than in dromaeosaurid and troodontid theropods.

If *Protarchaeopteryx* and *Caudipteryx* were flightless birds, they would presumably have lost the power of flight fairly soon (geologically speaking) after flight had been acquired by the earliest birds, which seems odd. However, there are many species of modern birds that have lost the power of flight, some fairly recently. These include the Galápagos cormorant; some grebes, ducks, and rails; and a parrot. My researches have shown that these secondarily flightless birds retain most of the features of their flying relatives, though their wings are often smaller. For example, among the flightless species I studied, all but one (*Atlantisia rogersi,* the Inaccessible Flightless Rail) had wing feathers with an asymmetrically placed rachis. Since flightless birds tend to retain their asymmetrical vanes, the presence of symmetrical ones in the wing feathers of *Protarchaeopteryx* and *Caudipteryx* suggests they have not secondarily lost the power of flight, but the evidence is equivocal. If these animals are not birds, why should they have evolved complex contour feathers like those of birds? There are two main and competing arguments to account for the evolution of contour feathers: either feathers evolved for thermal insulation or they evolved for flight.

Mammals and birds, being warm-blooded, have their bodies covered by insulation—fur and feathers. This insulation reduces heat losses from the body and can also protect the body from excess solar radiation. The relatively simple down feathers of birds would seem to fill this role very adequately. Indeed, the best sleeping bags are filled with down feathers because of their superior insulatory properties. In this regard down feathers are better than contour feathers. The reason down feathers are so effective is that they trap so much air, and air, being such a poor heat conductor, is an excellent insulator. The same principle lies behind the insulatory properties of fur, and of a variety of synthetic building materials like fiberglass batten and Styrofoam sheets. The superior insulatory properties of down feathers would appear to rule out the possibility that the more complex contour feathers evolved for insulation. However, while down feathers are ideal for passive insulation, animals must be able to adjust the thickness of their coats to suit external conditions. Their lack of stiffness makes down feathers unsuitable for this role.

When it is cold birds ruffle up their plumage and mammals fluff up their fur, thereby increasing the thickness of their insulation. The reverse happens when it is hot. These adjustments are effected by a small muscle that attaches to the base of each hair and to each contour feather. When the muscle contracts, the hair or feather becomes more erect, increasing the thickness of the layer of insulation. This explains why we get goose bumps when we are cold—a legacy of our more hirsute ancestry. When a bird erects its stiff contour feathers, the underlying down feathers tend to fluff up, filling the gaps with an increased thickness of the trapped air.

Having an erectile insulatory structure adequately accounts for the evolution of stiff feathers, but why do they need to be so elaborate? Would not a simple unbranched structure be just as good? Feathers are made of a protein called keratin, which also forms hair, scales, claws, and horns. Keratin is not a good heat conductor, and is therefore a fairly adequate insulator. Therefore, a covering of simple strips of keratin, each of which could be erected, would provide a modest insulatory layer. However, if the strips had bristly edges, the insulation would be improved because the bristles would trap a fringing layer of air. And the longer the bristles were, the wider would be this fringe. Further improvements could be made by having progressively finer bristles, and by these having side branches. It is therefore not difficult to visualize how barbs (bristles) and barbules (side branches) may have developed during the evolution of contour feathers. Later developments, including an asymmetrically placed rachis and a curved profile for the vane, could have modified the feathers for flight.

All of this is entirely speculative, but it does offer a logical explanation for why contour feathers may have evolved in animals that did not fly. According to this view, *Protarchaeopteryx* and *Caudipteryx* are not birds, but the flightless descendants of nonflying ancestors. Opponents of the idea that birds are theropods would argue that these animals are simply birds that have lost the power of flight. This raises the question of how birds should be defined. This was once a simple matter of the possession of feathers, but the discovery of so many new fossils has blurred the line between birds and nonbirds. This persuades me that birds really are theropods. The alternate viewpoint, that the similarities between birds and theropods are all due to convergence, is less convincing, especially as no other likely bird ancestor appears in the fossil record.

I still think it useful to retain the terms *birds* and *dinosaurs,* rather than using the terms *avian dinosaurs* and *non-avian dinosaurs*. I will therefore use the words *dinosaur* and *bird* below, according to common usage. Similarly, I will use the term *reptile,* even though this is not a monophyletic group.

Whatever one's views on avian origins, the fact remains that a chicken skeleton, especially an immature one, is sufficiently similar to that of a dinosaur to make it possible to convert the one into a realistic model of the other. And that will be our task in the next section.

Part 2

How to Build a
Tyrannosaurus Skeleton

▼▼▼

For the old hands who have already built a dinosaur from chicken bones, the explanations that follow on how to obtain the bones will be familiar. The only thing that has changed here is the selection of bones to be saved, so pay particular attention to this aspect. When it comes to marking up the bones for cutting and shaping, we will use cutout templates for the skull, pelvis, and shoulders. This saves the bother of measuring distances on the bones. Much of their shaping is done with a small file, which is something new too. The students at the high school in Colorado who had built a herd of *Apatosaurus,* and then a herd of *Tyrannosaurus* using the first draft of this book, had some great ideas, including some on glues. Various other ideas and suggestions from other dinosaur builders will also be included.

▼▼▼ Collecting the Chicken Bones

You will need four whole chickens to build your dinosaur (this will give you plenty of spare bones in case of mishaps), together with an additional part from another chicken (explained further on page 49). These need to be young chickens whose skeletons have not fully matured. Chicken take-out restaurants use young birds—so they are good and tender—and these are ideal, but be sure to specify that you don't want it cut up. All you need to do is save all the bones (including the legs and wings) from your meal, seal them in a plastic bag, and keep them in the freezer. Try to keep the bones of the various parts together as much as possible (such as all the bones of the left leg) using plastic wrap or foil. This will make it much easier for you later on.

Home-cooked chickens are fine too, provided they are young enough. The small chickens sold in supermarkets for baking and frying are young birds, and these are excellent. For example, I purchased a couple of small chickens the other day, one weighing 2.74 lb (1.25 kg), the other 3.84 lb (1.75 kg), and both were perfect for the job. But beware of stewing hens! No matter how small they are, their skeletons are fully mature, so many of their bones are already fused together. Stewing hens are therefore to be avoided.

If you are really keen to get started, you could buy four small chickens from a supermarket rather than waiting to accumulate four skeletons. You can then bake or boil the chickens whole; there are some recipes in an appendix that you might like to try. But before getting started, you should get together all the other things you need to build your dinosaur.

You'll need:

- the bones from four whole chickens, kept separate, and an extra hindquarter (as explained on page 49)
- a saucepan
- nail clippers of the pincer type
- a needle file. These are small, narrow files, not to be mistaken for nail files, which are much broader; I bought a set of different shaped needle files from my local hardware store for only a few dollars.
- a nail file or emery board
- nail scissors, preferably old
- tweezers

- a pair of dividers. These are like a compass but instead of having a pencil and a point they have two points; you can use a compass instead of dividers (from an office- or school-supplies store).
- a wire coat hanger
- pliers for cutting the coat hanger
- an old toothbrush
- a plastic mesh scouring pad
- a table knife
- a teaspoon
- a dinner plate
- floral tape (green wax tape, from a craft shop or florist)
- some pipe cleaners (6 inches or 15 cm long)
- sandpaper
- a roll of plastic twist ties (from a craft shop or garden supplier)
- plastic sandwich bags
- paper towels or toilet tissue
- toothpicks
- cotton swabs, such as Q-Tips
- masking tape
- a tube of clear glue or cement, such as Uhu
- Krazy Glue
- Spackle, Polyfilla, or plaster of paris
- white plasticine
- a dish rag or J-cloth
- an X-Acto knife or scalpel
- a piece of wood, approximately 2 feet long by 5 inches wide and 3/4 inch deep (60 cm by 10 cm by 2 cm). This is for the base of the stand. A piece of wooden molding from a lumber shop works well. Some shops supply pieces of finished wood as "craft board"; these are ideal.
- ten paper plates
- a few disposable cups
- a pencil and some index cards for making labels

- a ruler with metric and British imperial units (British imperial is the standard American measure)
- a Magic Marker
- a small plastic garbage or grocery bag
- a watercolor paint set (I purchased a small set from a toy shop for a dollar or less)

Optional extras:
- safety glasses for use with Krazy Glue
- a 60-watt table lamp, preferably with a metal shade
- an electric drill
- two empty tuna or other shallow cans
- two cupfuls of sand
- liquid laundry bleach
- a small hacksaw, from a craft shop
- spray paint for an overall finish

A Note on Glues

Two glues are recommended by the Colorado group. The first has a trade name of Hot Stuff (Zap is similar, and is available in Canada). It is like Krazy Glue, but it comes in a larger and more convenient bottle, and you can get an accelerator for it. All you have to do is add a droplet of Hot Stuff or Zap to the bones being glued, then spray on the accelerator. The glue sets instantly. The second glue, called Quick Tite, is used for gluing false fingernails in place, and is available at cosmetic counters. It, too, is like Krazy Glue, but has the advantage of being in a really convenient applicator bottle. All of these glues—Hot Stuff, Zap, Quick Tite, and regular Krazy Glue, are cyanoacrylates, and all work the same way. That means you can use accelerator for all of them. Now that I've tried using accelerator, I can see why my friends in Colorado are so keen on it—it causes instant bonding. But it is expensive ($10 in Canada). It also gives off fumes, so it must be used with good ventilation, and sparingly. Indeed, I recommend restricting the use of the Krazy Glue to those jobs where you really need it. Use the old-fashioned clear glue, like Uhu, everywhere else (you can use it throughout if you want to). A glue like Uhu—which smells like nail varnish and is used in building plastic models—has several advantages: it can bridge gaps; it forms stronger unions, primarily because it can be built up, in layers, over joints; and it is more forgiving and more user friendly. Youngsters should certainly not use Krazy Glue. White glues like Elmer's are not very good for this type of project because they do not have much strength. Some people have told me that hot glue from a glue gun works really well, especially when tacking bones together.

The measurements used in this book are in British imperial units and metric units. Scientists always employ metric units, which are much easier to use, and in some parts of the book, where precise measurements are required, only metric units are given. As in the first part of the book, when important terms are used for the first time they are printed in bold. Anatomical directions will be used for orientations, namely: **anterior** (front), **posterior** (back), **dorsal** (top), **ventral** (bottom), **lateral** (outside), **medial** (inside).

Anatomical orientations.

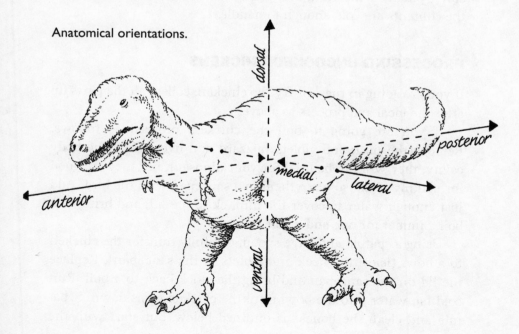

▼▼▼ Boiling Up the Bones

It is easiest to boil and process one chicken at a time, at least to start with. Once you've completed one chicken, you might want to try processing the other three at the same time. If you decide to do this, boil them up in separate saucepans, so that their bones do not become mixed. All chicken carcasses need boiling, even if they have been previously cooked. If you are starting with an uncooked chicken and decide to boil it rather than bake it (boiling gives best results), follow the procedure as set out below. This will yield chicken stock for making soup, as well as meat for some other meals. Recipes are given in an appendix.

PROCESSING PREVIOUSLY COOKED CHICKENS

Place the chicken carcass into a saucepan, cover with water, and boil for one to one and a half hours. Do not overboil or the bones will become too brittle. If your chicken was baked in the oven, boil it for only an hour. Then remove the saucepan from the stove, put it in the sink, and gently flush with cold water until the contents are cold enough to handle.

PROCESSING UNCOOKED CHICKENS

If you are going to roast or fry the chicken, collect all the parts up after the meal and process as above.

If you are going to boil the chicken, proceed as follows. Remove the neck and giblets (gizzard and liver) from the body cavity; they will not be used for your dinosaur, but they are good for making stock, so place them in a saucepan with the bird. Add just enough water to cover the bird, close the lid, and bring to a boil. Simmer for one and a half hours.

Using a spatula and large spoon, carefully transfer the chicken to a bowl (leave the neck and giblets in the saucepan). Replace the lid on the saucepan and bring the stock back to a boil. Run cold tap water into the bowl until the chicken cools down. Separate and clean the bones, as outlined below, but start with the wings and legs. Save the meat in a plastic freezer bag, refrigerating for later use (see recipe appendix). Return all other soft parts and unwanted bones to the saucepan as they are removed.

Allow the stock to simmer for at least an hour, then strain off into a bowl. Cover the bowl (to exclude bacteria) while the chicken stock cools to room temperature, then transfer to the refrigerator. Once chilled, the solidified fat is easily removed from the top. Transfer the gelatinous stock to a freezer bag, seal and label, and store in the freezer until needed.

▼▼▼ Separating and Cleaning the Bones

This involves separating the bones, removing the remnants of meat, washing, and leaving them to dry.

Be gentle when handling the bones, because many of them are fragile and easy to break. As each bone is removed, clean it by rinsing with water. Remove any remaining scraps of meat by gently scrubbing with the toothbrush. Pieces of cartilage (gristle) can be removed from the ends of the long bones (bones of the legs and wings) by scrubbing with the plastic scouring pad. As is true of all vertebrates, most of a chicken's skeleton is formed of cartilage during the early stages of development. As development proceeds, the cartilage becomes **ossified**; that is, it is replaced by bone. The ends of bones are the last to ossify, hence the caps of cartilage at the ends of the long bones.

You'll need to identify the bones as they are removed, but don't worry, you'll be told how to do this. Once you've identified a bone, label it so you can find it by name later on.

Sometimes you will be told to note whether the bone is from the left or right side.

To make a label, cut a piece of card about an inch (3 cm) square, and write the information in pencil. Writing in pencil is the easiest way of making a permanent record, and has been used for many years for labeling pickled specimens in museums. Ink, on the other hand, runs, and soon becomes illegible. Make a small hole in the label with the point of your scissors and attach

DIRE WARNING! ▼▼▼ Cats and dogs love chicken bones, even scrubbed and dried ones that look totally unappetizing. Therefore keep all bones, and skeletons, out of the way of your pets. Josh, one of the Colorado students, built a *T. rex* skeleton that he named Richard. Unfortunately his dog ate the whole thing, so he built Richard II. Can you believe it, that king was deposed too! Undaunted, Josh set to work and built Richard III. *You have been warned.*

it to the bone with a length of twist tie. Sometimes a label will be placed beside a group of similar bones, or enclosed inside a plastic bag of bones, instead of labeling each separately. Leave the cleaned and labeled bones to dry on paper plates lined with paper towels or tissue. The scraps of meat and gristle, together with unwanted bones, can be added to the stock in the saucepan or disposed of in the garbage bag.

STEP 1: SEPARATING AND CLEANING THE BONES OF THE BOILED CARCASS

Note: If this is a previously uncooked chicken, begin by removing the wings and legs.

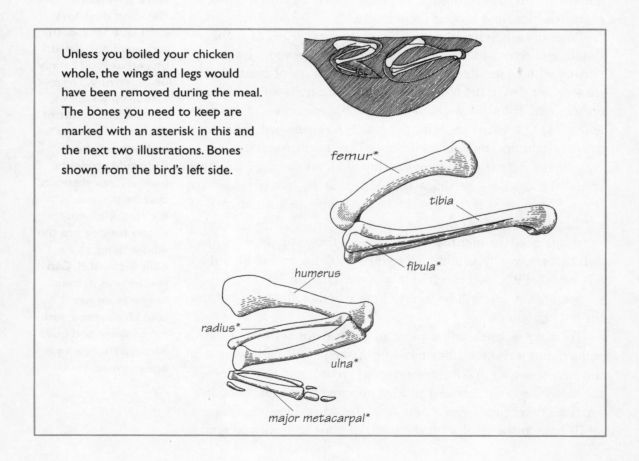

Unless you boiled your chicken whole, the wings and legs would have been removed during the meal. The bones you need to keep are marked with an asterisk in this and the next two illustrations. Bones shown from the bird's left side.

femur*

tibia

fibula*

humerus

radius*

ulna*

major metacarpal*

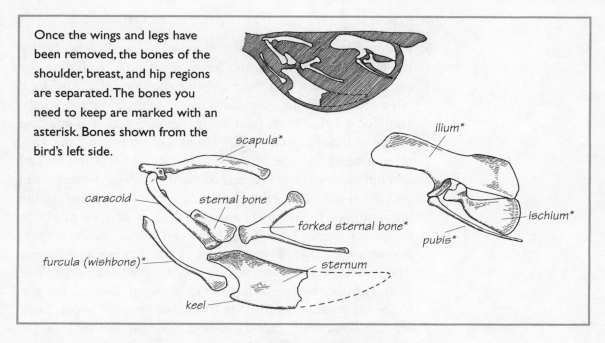

Once the wings and legs have been removed, the bones of the shoulder, breast, and hip regions are separated. The bones you need to keep are marked with an asterisk. Bones shown from the bird's left side.

scapula*

ilium*

caracoid

sternal bone

forked sternal bone*

ischium*

pubis*

furcula (wishbone)*

sternum

keel

1: Lay the remains of the chicken on the dinner plate and locate the breast region.

2: Using your fingers, remove the loose meat from the side of the rib cage to uncover the shoulder. The **pectoral girdle** (shoulder) is in two parts. The upper part, the **scapula** (shoulder blade), is long and slender and is attached to the ribs by muscles. The lower part, the **coracoid**, is thicker and shorter, and is firmly attached to the front of the **sternum** (breastbone). Birds, unlike most other tetrapods, have the pectoral girdle rigidly attached to the rest of the skeleton. This is to give a firm anchorage for the flapping wings.

3: Lift the scapula so that it comes free from the rib cage—it will come away very easily. Separate the scapula from the coracoid, which may require more effort. Save the scapula, noting on the label from which side of the body it came (from the chicken's perspective). Free the coracoid from the sternum—you may have to pull a little harder than you did to free the scapula. Discard the coracoid.

4: Repeat step 2 for the other side of the chicken.

5: Remove the sternum, which is attached to the rib cage. Notice the large vertical flange, the **keel**. Most birds, including the chicken, are fliers, and their deeply keeled sternum provides a large attachment area for the muscles that power the wings. Look for a forked bone (about 2 inches or 5 cm long) attached to the anterior dorsal region (front top corner) of the sternum. There is one on either side. We'll call these the **forked sternal bones**. They are part of the developing sternum, and will eventually fuse with the main part of that bone as the bird matures. Immediately anterior to the forked sternal bone is another sternal bone. Like the forked sternal bones, there is one on either side. They are part of the developing sternum. The forked sternal bones will be used for the pectoral girdle of your *Tyrannosaurus*, so they are to be saved. Discard the rest of the sternum, including the (unforked) sternal bones. Look for the wishbone (furcula). We'll use this for part of the dinosaur's tail.

6: Remove the ribs from one side of the vertebral column. You'll probably find six ribs on either side, each with a forked end where it articulates with its corresponding vertebra. (**Note:** the first rib is not forked, but expanded at the top end—it is also fairly straight and flat). Be gentle when removing the ribs, because it is easy to break them at the top, where they are attached. Keep the ribs from the left and right sides separate. Some of the ribs are attached at their lower end to a second bone, which attaches to the sternum. These bones are called **sternal ribs**, to distinguish them from the **vertebral ribs** (true ribs). There are five pairs of sternal ribs. Some of the sternal ribs will be used for making the forelimbs. Using a Magic Marker, divide a paper plate into three equal segments, labeling these *left vertebral ribs, right vertebral ribs,* and *sacral ribs.* Save all the ribs, placing them into their appropriate segments.

Humans also have sternal ribs, but they remain cartilaginous—that is, the gristly cartilage is not replaced by bone during growth and development. Ossification of the sternal ribs in birds has to do with their unique breathing mechanism.

As you clean each rib, you will notice a small cartilaginous process, or projecting part, about halfway down its length on the posterior edge. As the chicken matures, this will ossify, forming the **uncinate process**. The uncinate process of one rib overlaps the rib behind it, increasing the rigidity of the rib cage.

7: Repeat step 6 for the other side.

At this point you are going to collect the vertebrae. You do not need the chicken's **cervical** (neck) vertebrae. They are easy to distinguish from the **thoracic** vertebrae, the ones to which the ribs were attached. Each thoracic, or back, vertebra has a large square bony plate, called the **neural spine**, whereas the cervical vertebrae lack this feature. Do the following:

1: Look carefully at the neck end and identify the cervical verte-brae—there will probably be about six of them (more if your chicken was purchased uncooked). Discard all of them.

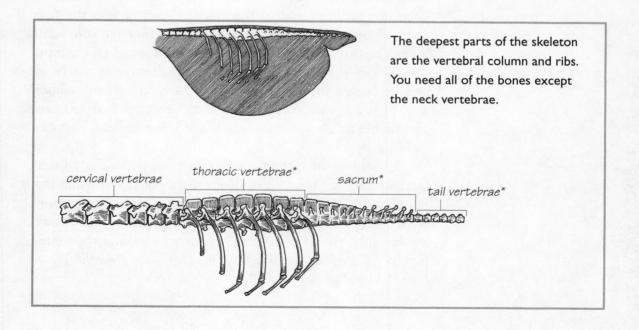

The deepest parts of the skeleton are the vertebral column and ribs. You need all of the bones except the neck vertebrae.

cervical vertebrae   thoracic vertebrae*   sacrum*   tail vertebrae*

2: Straighten an 8-inch (20 cm) length of plastic twist tie. Starting at the front end, thread this through the centers of the vertebrae. This is to keep them all together and in the right order. The idea is to feed the plastic twist tie through the **neural canal** of each vertebra, the channel that conveys the spinal cord. You will probably be able to see the spinal cord as a fairly thick white thread, and this will give you a target to aim for. You should be able to push the twist tie all the way along the vertebral column, as far as the beginning of the **pelvic girdle** (pelvis). Remove the meat and sinews from the vertebral column and see where it joins the pelvic girdle. Gently break the vertebral column from the pelvic girdle at this point. You may have some difficulty separating the vertebrae, because the last two—those immediately anterior to the pelvic girdle—are quite firmly united to the anterior end of the **sacrum**, the series of fused vertebrae to which the pelvic girdle is attached. Once you have separated the vertebral column, you should be able to thread the twist tie all the way through. If there are still one or two vertebrae attaching to the anterior end of the pelvic girdle, gently try to break them free. Add them to the twist tie, without changing their orientation. Label the anterior end of the vertebral series. Join the two ends of the twist tie to secure the vertebrae. If you were unable to thread the twist tie through the vertebral column, just remove the vertebrae one at a time, starting at the front end, removing the meat as you go. As each vertebra comes free, thread it onto the twist tie. Whichever method you use, you should finish up with about six or seven vertebrae on the twist tie.

The individual vertebrae can now be separated from one another and scrubbed clean of meat and cartilage, using the toothbrush. When clean, label this string *thoracic vertebrae.* Attach the label to the front end, so as to record which way around they go. (If you forget which way around the vertebrae go, there's an easy way of checking—see *How the Vertebrae Fit Together,* on page 76.)

The Vertebral Column

Different regions of the vertebral column are modified for different functions, and this shows in the specialization of the individual vertebrae. This regional specialization is especially marked in mammals and birds, less so in reptiles. Mammals are conservative in the numbers of vertebrae in each region. There are always seven cervical vertebrae, even in the giraffe[*] with its long neck; usually twelve to fourteen thoracics, which articulate with the ribs (the horse is one exception, with eighteen, sometimes nineteen thoracics); five to seven lumbars, which have no ribs but prominent transverse processes; three to five sacrals, which are fused into the sacrum; and a variable number of caudals.

Birds have especially long and flexible necks, with fourteen cervical vertebrae. The trunk region, in contrast, is both short and stiff. There are only four or five thoracic vertebrae, and these are rigidly joined together. The thoracic vertebrae are firmly united with the **synsacrum**. The synsacrum comprises about twelve vertebrae firmly fused together. The first five or six vertebrae are equivalent to the lumbar vertebrae of a mammal, the next two are equivalent to the sacral vertebrae, while the last five or six are equivalent to the anterior caudal vertebrae. The moveable part of a bird's tail is very short, comprising six free caudal vertebrae and a terminal bone that is flattened from side to side, which is called the pygostyle. The entire tail is enclosed inside the "parson's nose," a moveable fleshy pad attached to the end of the sacrum.

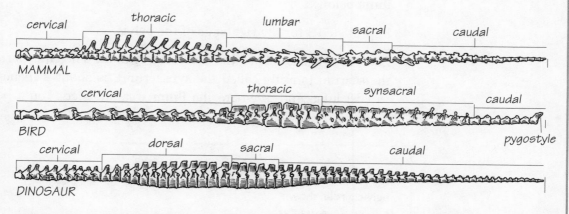

The vertebral columns of a mammal (*top*), a bird (*middle*), and a reptile (*bottom*), to show the names used for the different regions.

[*]Some question has been raised about the neck vertebrae of the giraffe. See the article by Solounias in Further Reading.

Reptiles have less specialized vertebral columns, with greater variability in the numbers of vertebrae in the different regions. The drawing depicts the vertebral column of *T. rex*. The dorsal vertebrae are equivalent to the thoracic and lumbar vertebrae of a mammal.

Your dinosaur's vertebral column is made from the chickens' thoracic and synsacral vertebrae—the chickens' cervical and caudal vertebrae are not used at all.

3: Find the pelvic girdle. Look at the left side first. If the hind leg is still attached, take it off and keep it for later. The pelvic girdle is in two halves, right and left, and each half is made up of three separate bones. The upper bone, the ilium, is about 3 inches long (7 cm). It is attached medially (on the inside) to part of the vertebral column. It is also attached to the two other bones that make up the pelvic girdle—the ischium, which is triangular, and the pubis, which is long and slender. Using your fingers, clear away the cartilage, thereby separating the ilium from the underlying vertebrae, and the ischium from the ilium and pubis. Save the ilium, ischium, and pubis, labeling each one. It is important to note to which side each ilium belongs.

4: Repeat step 3 for the right side of the pelvis.

5: Look at what is left of the vertebral column. The first part, the sacrum (strictly called the synsacrum), is about 2 inches (5 cm) long, and is where the ilium was attached. You'll be

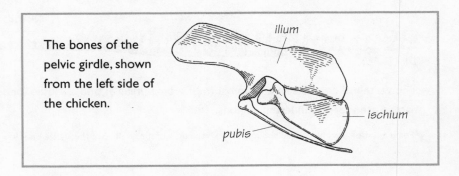

The bones of the pelvic girdle, shown from the left side of the chicken.

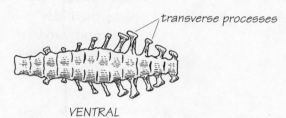

The sacrum, removed from the rest of the vertebral column, shown from the left side (*top*) and from beneath (*bottom*). Notice the long processes on the most posterior vertebrae.

ANTERIOR

LATERAL

transverse processes

VENTRAL

able to count up to eleven or twelve vertebrae, and these are firmly joined together, making the sacrum rigid. The parson's nose is attached to the end of the sacrum.

6: Remove the parson's nose and discard it.

7: Simmer the sacrum in a small covered saucepan for an hour, checking periodically to make sure it does not boil dry. This is to soften the joints between the individual vertebrae, making them easier to separate. Remove the sacrum from the saucepan and allow it to cool. Look at it. You'll see that the vertebrae at the posterior end have large **transverse processes**, the bony protrusions that extend from either side of each vertebra. There should be eleven or twelve vertebrae. Using a knife, strip off the plastic covering from a 10-inch (25 cm) length of plastic twist tie, freeing the wire. Thread the wire through the neural canals of the vertebrae, as you did for the other vertebrae, twisting the two ends together to form a loop. Carefully clear away any remaining soft parts with the toothbrush.

Using gentle finger pressure, try separating the two vertebrae at either end of the sacrum, taking care not to break off any bony processes. They will probably come free, and you may be able to remove one or two others, but the rest will probably have to be cut apart. Lay the sacrum down on a damp dishrag, ventral surface up, so that the **neural spines**, the bony processes that project from the top of the vertebrae, face away from you. Notice the obvious suture lines between adjacent vertebrae. Starting at the anterior end of the sacrum, place the blade point of an X-Acto knife (or scalpel) on the first suture and gently work it down one side. Repeat for the other side. It may help to try and lever the partially freed vertebra away from the rest by twisting the blade slightly. Once you have separated the vertebra, repeat the process for the next one.

WARNING ▼▼▼
Youngsters should not use an X-Acto knife or scalpel without an adult helper.

Notice how the neural canal rapidly expands in diameter in the sacral region. Indeed, it becomes so large that it encroaches upon the main body of each vertebra (called the **centrum**), which becomes reduced to a ring of bone. The reason for this expansion is explained in *The Sacral Swelling,* on the next page.

The first few vertebrae have fairly prominent neural spines, but the next two or three have very short ones, and short transverse processes. These vertebrae will not be used, so do not bother trying to separate them. Undo the wire and remove the first few vertebrae (those with fairly prominent neural spines), making sure not to change their order or direction. Remove the unwanted (fused together) vertebrae and discard them. Replace the vertebrae with the fairly prominent neural spines. Twist the two ends of the wire together again. Go to the other end of the sacrum and start separating the ones with the prominent transverse processes.

Don't worry if some of the sacral vertebrae break during the process—you'll be very lucky if you can separate them all without some mishaps! Save all the vertebrae, including those that are not too badly broken—they can be repaired with glue when they are dry. You should finish up with half a dozen or more separate vertebrae on the wire. Label the string *sacral vertebrae,* noting which is the anterior end. Place it on your vertebrae plate.

The Sacral Swelling

Stegosaurus and several other dinosaurs are often credited with having two brains: one in the usual place, and the other in the sacral region. Although untrue—these dinosaurs, like all other vertebrates, had only one brain—there was a considerable enlargement of the spinal cord in the sacral region. This is shown by the large size of the neural canals in the sacral region. In *Stegosaurus,* the partially fused sacral vertebrae form a bony cavity with a volume that is about twenty times larger than that of the braincase.

All tetrapods have a spinal enlargement in the sacral region, including humans, though these are nowhere near as prominent as in *Stegosaurus*. There is also a second spinal swelling, in the shoulder region.

The spinal column gives off paired spinal nerves, left and right, all the way down the vertebral column, and these exit between adjacent vertebrae. The spinal nerves are about the same thickness all the way down the backbone—about as thick as a pencil in humans. However, they become enlarged and joined together in the shoulder and sacral regions, and the spinal cord is similarly enlarged. The reason for the increased complexity has to do with controlling the arms and the legs.

The usual explanation for the sacral swelling of the spinal cord in dinosaurs like *Stegosaurus* is that it was associated with the nervous control of the massive back legs and spiked tail. However, this may be only part of the story. Birds, as you have seen for yourself, have an extensive sacral swelling, but this cannot be attributed solely to increased neurological function. In addition to housing the bird's spinal cord, the bony cavity accommodates a large structure called the **glycogen body**, of uncertain function. Perhaps the same was also true for some of its dinosaurian relatives.

STEP 2: SEPARATING AND CLEANING THE BONES OF THE LEGS

Find the two back legs—chances are the individual bones are still joined together by **ligaments** (tough sinews that connect bones to bones; **tendons** are similar, but they connect muscles to bones). Do the following for each leg:

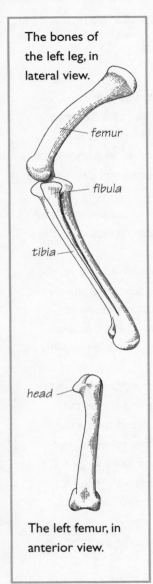

The bones of the left leg, in lateral view.

femur

fibula

tibia

head

The left femur, in anterior view.

1: Identify the femur (thighbone)—it is shorter than the tibia (shinbone). Keeping the two bones still attached at the knee joint, remove the meat from the femur. You'll notice a distinct knob at the upper end. This knob, called the **head of the femur**, fits into the hip socket.

In adults, each end of the femur is formed of bone, but in young birds, it is made of cartilage. This cartilage forms a cap at each end of the bone, and provides for its growth. The extent of the cartilaginous cap therefore gives you an idea of the age of your particular chicken. For example, if the cartilage cap is large and easily comes away from the bone, you can be sure that you were eating a tender young chicken. You'll find similar caps at the ends of the tibia too.

2: With the femur still attached, clear away the meat from the tibia, starting at the knee. Watch out for a slender bone, the fibula, which runs along the outside of the tibia. Once you've found the fibula, you'll be able to tell which leg you've got. This is because the fibula is always on the outside, and the head of the femur is always on the inside. Make a label to show which leg is which.

3: Remove the rest of the meat and other soft parts to separate the three bones (femur, tibia, fibula). Discard the tibia. Remove the cartilaginous caps from the ends of the femur. They may come off easily, but if not, remove them by scrubbing with the plastic scouring pad. If you've got an older bird, and the caps of cartilage do not come off easily with scrubbing, leave them attached. Clean and label the two femora and fibulae.

STEP 3: SEPARATING AND CLEANING THE BONES OF THE WINGS

Find the remains of the two wings—chances are that the individual bones are still joined together by ligaments. Do the following for each wing:

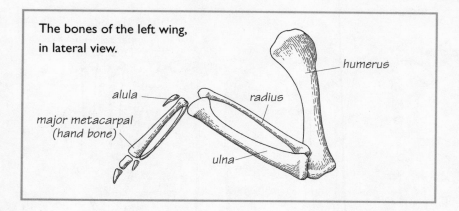

The bones of the left wing, in lateral view.

1: Clearing away the meat as you go, identify the **humerus** (upper arm bone), and the two lower arm bones, the **radius** and **ulna**. The radius is about half as thick as the ulna, and is straight. Discard the humerus.

2: At the far end of the lower arm you'll see a small projection— this is the bird's thumb, called the **alula**. The alula functions in flight as an antistalling device. You can often see the alula being deployed when watching pigeons coming in to land. The alula, which looks like a small wing, pops out from the leading edge of the wing just before the pigeon lands.

Although you don't need to keep the chicken's thumb, you do need one of the two bones that lie next to the thumb. These bones, which are a little over an inch long (3 cm), are like the palm of our hand. These hand bones, called **metacarpals**, become fused together with maturity. One of the hand bones, the **major metacarpal**, is much thicker than the other, and is also straight. It is the only hand bone we need to keep. Discard the rest of the hand. Clean and label the bones that are needed, labeling them as *radius, ulna,* and *hand bone.* There is no need to distinguish left from right.

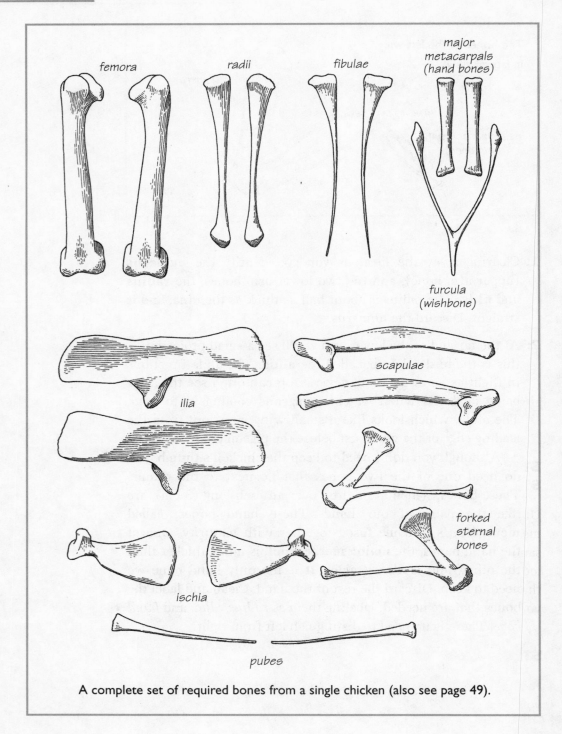

A complete set of required bones from a single chicken (also see page 49).

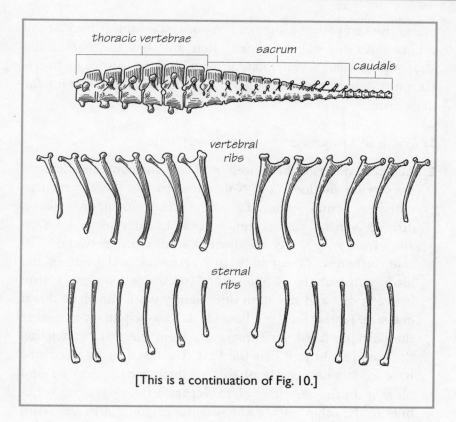

thoracic vertebrae

sacrum

caudals

vertebral ribs

sternal ribs

[This is a continuation of Fig. 10.]

STEP 4: CHECKING THE SAUCEPAN FOR STRAY BONES

Unless you boiled a whole chicken, you'll find scraps of skin, meat, ligaments, and cartilage left behind on the bottom of the saucepan. But there may also be some bones that you've overlooked. Pour off most of the water, which will be cold, and feel through the scraps to find any stray bones. Check any bones that you find against the drawings to see whether it is needed.

STEP 5: THE ADDITIONAL SACRUM

In addition to the bones obtained from your four whole chickens, you need an extra sacrum. This can be obtained from the appropriate chicken part at a supermarket or restaurant. (Check at the supermarket for a leg segment that still has the back bone attached; or search your plate after a chicken dinner to find a sacrum.) Remove the unwanted bones, then do the following for the sacrum:

1: Boil it in a saucepan of water for one hour.

2: Add cold water to the saucepan to cool the contents. Remove the sacrum and look at it. Notice the anterior sacral vertebrae with the neural spines. Lay the sacrum down on a damp dishrag, ventral surface up, so that the neural spines face away from you. Notice the obvious suture lines between adjacent vertebrae. Count back five vertebrae and position the blade point of the X-Acto knife (or scalpel) on the suture between this and the sixth one. Gently work the blade down one side. Repeat for the other side. It may help to try and lever the partially freed vertebrae away from the rest by twisting the blade slightly. When the first five fused sacral vertebrae have been removed, label this segment *partial sacrum* and place it on the vertebrae plate. Separate the remaining vertebrae in the other part of the sacrum, as you did in step 7 on page 43. Strip a short length (about 4 inches or 10 cm) of plastic twist tie. Thread the freed sacral vertebrae onto the wire, in order, twisting the two ends together. Label these *sacral vertebrae*—there should be six or seven of them—and place them on the vertebrae plate.

Bone Discoloration

WARNING ▼▼▼
Youngsters should not use bleach without an adult helper.

If any of your bones are discolored, they can be restored to a more natural bone white by using bleach. Make up an approximately 10 percent solution by adding a quarter cup of liquid bleach to one pint of cold water. Leave the bones to soak in the solution for about ten minutes. Rinse them off under a running tap and leave them to dry.

▼▼▼ Preparing the Bones for Mounting

In this section you'll choose all the bones you need to make your *Tyrannosaurus* skeleton from your four sets of chicken bones and the additional sacrum. You'll group them according to different parts of the dinosaur's skeleton, placing each group of bones on its own paper plate to keep them separate. For future reference, these are listed below:

THE PLATES AND THEIR CONTENTS

Skull 2 pairs of ilia, 3 ischia (one of which is the largest one you can find), and one scapula

Teeth Up to 6 small flat unforked ribs, 4 fibulae, 6 pubes

Vertebrae 4 strings labeled *thoracic vertebrae* and 4 strings labeled *sacral vertebrae.* There is also part of a sacrum labeled *partial sacrum,* a short string of 6 or 7 vertebrae labeled *sacral vertebrae,* 2 furculae, and 2 radii.

Pelvis 1 pair of ilia, 1 pair of ischia, 1 pair of forked sternal bones

Hind legs and feet The thinnest pair of femora, 2 ulnae, 2 radii, 2 hand bones, 2 fibulae, 6 forked sternal bones

Ribs Plate is divided into three equal segments, labeled *left vertebral ribs, right vertebral ribs, sternal ribs.* There should be up to 12 left and 12 right vertebral ribs, and up to 14 sternal ribs.

Pectoral girdle and limbs 1 pair of forked sternal bones, 6 sternal ribs

Spare parts Remnants of the forked sternal bones, at least 1 pair of fibulae, at least 4 sternal ribs that are about 15 mm long and have a round rather than a flat cross section

You will also be modifying some of the bones by cutting and gluing, to make them look more like those of *Tyrannosaurus.*

While many of the chicken bones will be used for making the same bone in the dinosaur, others will be used differently. The chicken's femur, for example, is used for the dinosaur's femur, but the dinosaur's tibia is made from the chicken's ulna. Here is a list of the different parts of the dinosaur, and the chicken bones that are used. (Note: for paired structures, like the pelvis, only the bones needed for one side are listed.):

Skull: 2 pairs of ilia, 3 ischia

Teeth: 4 fibulae, 4 flat ribs, 4 pubes

Vertebral column: 4 strings of thoracics, 4 strings of sacrals, one partial sacrum, one short string of sacrals, 2 furculae, 2 radii

ribs: ribs

femur: femur

tibia: ulna

fibula: radius

metatarsus: 1 hand bone, 1 radius

hind foot (toes): 3 forked sternal bones, 1 fibula

reversed hallux: remains of the fibula used in the rest of the foot

pelvis: 1 ilium, 1 ischium, 1 forked sternal bone

scapulocoracoid: remnant of forked sternal bone left over from making the feet

humerus: 1 sternal rib

radius: 1 sternal rib

ulna: 1 sternal rib

hand: fibula

You will have plenty of spare bones. For example, you need only one pair of femora, but you have at least four pairs. However, other bones, like the vertebrae, will be in shorter supply. The leftover bones will be kept together as spare parts, in case you have any accidents during the cutting and gluing stages.

STEP 1: PUTTING THE BONES IN ORDER

1: Look at the vertebral ribs on the ribs plate. There will be up to twenty-four for each side. See if you can find some vertebral ribs that are not forked. These are fairly straight and flat and may be only about an inch (2.5 cm) or so long. They are unsuitable for making your dinosaur's ribs and will be used instead for making some of the teeth. Place them onto a paper plate labeled *teeth*.

The unforked vertebral ribs are used for making teeth.

2: If you are not sure which ribs are left and which are right, check by picking up a forked rib and having a close look at it. Notice how curved it is. Also notice that the forked end has a long branch and a short branch. Lay the rib down on the table with the forked end furthest away from you and the short branch touching the surface. The long branch will be pointing up toward you, as illustrated. Does the concave side of the rib face left or right? If it faces left, the rib is from the left side, as shown in the illustration.

Your dinosaur needs thirteen pairs of ribs. However, to make dinosaur ribs, some of the vertebral ribs need to be extended in length by adding parts of other ribs, so you need more than just thirteen pairs. Keep them all on the ribs plate for now, together with the sternal ribs.

3: Check the vertebrae plate. There should be four strings labeled *thoracic vertebrae* and four strings labeled *sacral vertebrae,* each with a label showing which end is anterior. There

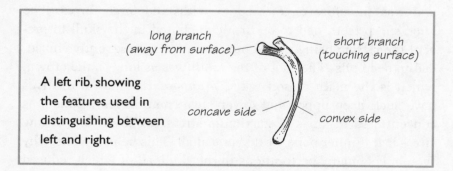

long branch
(away from surface)

short branch
(touching surface)

A left rib, showing the features used in distinguishing between left and right.

concave side

convex side

is also an additional short string, labeled *sacral vertebrae,* and a short series of fused sacrals, labeled *partial sacrum.*

Add two of the six wishbones and two of the six radii to the plate. These bones will be cut up and used as terminal tail vertebrae.

4: Put two pairs of ilia, three ischia (one of which is the largest one you can find), and one scapula onto a different paper plate and label it *skull.*

5: Put four fibulae and six pubes onto the teeth plate (which already has the unforked vertebral ribs).

6: Put one pair of forked sternal bones and six sternal ribs onto another plate and label it *pectoral girdle and limbs.*

7: Put one pair of ilia, one pair of ischia, and one pair of forked sternal bones onto a plate labeled *pelvis.*

8: Choose the thinnest pair of femora and put them onto a plate labeled *hind legs and feet.* Add two ulnae, two radii, two hand bones, two fibulae, and six forked sternal bones.

9: Put all the bones left over onto a plate labeled *spare parts.*

▼▼▼ Building the Skull

The skull is the most impressive part of the entire animal. It was used for biting and tearing through the bodies of other animals, and was therefore engineered to withstand large forces. The long, sharp teeth had to be firmly anchored in the skull to prevent them from being ripped out, and were consequently embedded in deep pits. The root of the tooth was as long as the crown, which is the main reason why *Tyrannosaurus* and its relatives have such deep upper and lower jaws (**mandibles**). Bone was concentrated in areas of maximum stress, while regions of low stress had thinner bone, or no bone at all. This helps explain why there are so many perforations in the skull, all of which reduced

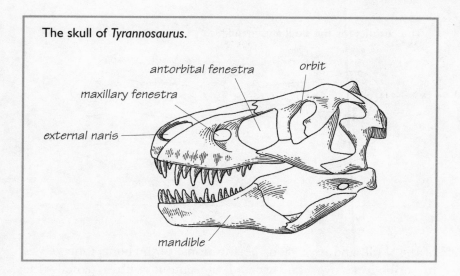

The skull of *Tyrannosaurus*.

antorbital fenestra

orbit

maxillary fenestra

external naris

mandible

its weight. Each perforation, or **fenestra** (Latin for *window*), has its own name, as shown in the drawing. Notice that what appears to be the **orbit** (eye socket) is in fact the **antorbital fenestra** (*ant-* in Latin means *before*). The orbit is bilobed, and the eye probably occupied the dorsal (upper) portion. The most anterior perforation is for the **external naris** (nostril). Posterior to this is the **maxillary fenestra**, named for the **maxilla** bone which it perforates.

Although the skull is the largest and most intricate part of the whole skeleton, it is fairly easy to build. All you have to do is follow the various stages, step by step, and you'll finish up with a magnificent-looking skull that you won't believe you built.

STEP 1: MARKING UP THE OUTLINE OF THE SKULL AND LOWER JAWS

All of the marking up on the bones will be done using cutouts, which you'll find on page 183 at the back of the book. Start by removing the cutouts page. Carefully cut around the outlines of the left and right halves of the skull. Do the same for the left and right halves of the lower jaw. Put the rest of the page somewhere safe for later use. There are two ways of transferring the outlines

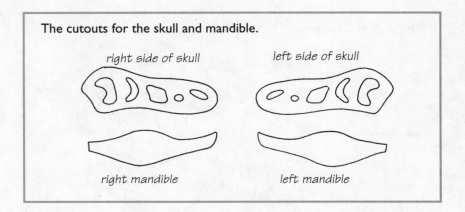

The cutouts for the skull and mandible.

right side of skull   *left side of skull*

right mandible   *left mandible*

of the skull, and its various perforations, to the bone. One way is to scribble all over the back of the cutout with a pencil—the graphite from the pencil will act like carbon paper. When you place the cutout against the bone and trace the picture on the printed side of the paper, the details will be transferred from the cutout to the bone. The other way is to use a pair of fine scissors, or the blade of an X-Acto knife, to cut out the perforations in the skull drawings. Then, using a sharp pencil, trace around all the cut edges, thereby transferring all of the details to the bone.

Tracing Method

Using a soft pencil (no harder than an HB), scribble on the reverse side of each of the skull cutouts, so as to cover the areas of each of the five perforations. Make sure that each patch of pencil scribble more than covers the outline of its corresponding perforation. Also, make sure that the patch is good and black.

Cutting-Out Method

WARNING ▼▼▼
Youngsters should not do this without an adult helper.

If you are using scissors, start by making a small hole on the edge of one of the five perforations with one of the points of the scissors. Using the hole as a start, carefully cut all the way around the edge of the perforation. Repeat for the other four perforations. If you are using an X-Acto knife, place the skull cutout onto a thick newspaper, so that you have many pages of paper beneath the blade. Pressing down firmly, follow around the outline of the first perforation with the tip of the blade, thereby cutting it out. Repeat for the other four perforations.

Find the paper plate labeled *skull*. This contains two pairs of ilia and three ischia. One pair of ilia will be used for the left and right sides of the skull. The other pair of ilia will be used for the two halves of the lower jaw. Two of the ischia will be used for filling in the skull roof, while the third, the largest, will fill the gap at the back of the skull. Add your four cutouts to the skull plate.

All of the bones have to be marked up prior to trimming and filing.

Start with the left side of the skull.

1: Find the left ilium. Lay it down flat on the table. (If you try to lay it down on its other side it will not lie flat.) When the ilium is lying flat, you are looking at it from the outside. The front of the ilium faces toward the left. Run a finger along the lateral (outside) surface. Notice that the anterior part of the ilium is hollow, while the posterior portion bulges out toward you. (If it's the other way around you've got the ilium from the right side—swap them over and start again.)

Notice the prominent ridge that runs obliquely across the ilium, separating the anterior hollow from the posterior bulge.

2: Find the cutout for the left side of the skull. Hold the cutout in place so that its posterior edge lines up with the posterior edge of the ilium. Adjust its position so that the antorbital fenestra and orbit lie on either side of the prominent ridge, as

The chicken's left ilium.

cutout for left side of skull

The chicken's left ilium with the cutout for the left side of the skull, ready for marking up.

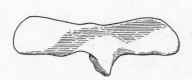

The chicken's right ilium.

cutout for right side of skull

The chicken's right ilium with the cutout for the right side of the skull, ready for marking up.

shown. The anterior tip of the cutout will lie in the middle of the anterior hollow.

3: Using a sharp pencil, trace around the outline of the cutout. There is no need to draw around the entire outline because there are parts where the edge of the ilium is sufficiently close to the cutout to make this unnecessary (for example, along most of the top of the skull and much of the ventral edge).

4: While still holding the cutout in place, trace around each of the perforations. You will need to press fairly hard with the tip of the pencil. Check to make sure that each outline has been transferred to the bone. Do this by lifting part of the cutout, taking care not to move the rest of it relative to the bone. You need only a faint mark on the surface, but it may be necessary to go over the outline several times to achieve this. When satisfied, remove the cutout and pencil over all the marks.

Repeat steps 1–4 for the right side.

Each half of the lower jaw is made from an ilium, but the left jaw is made from the right ilium, and vice versa.

Start with the left half of the lower jaw.

1: Find the right ilium. Lay it down flat on the table, as you did when marking up the skull. However, place it upside down so that the ventral process is uppermost, as shown. Notice that

The chicken's right ilium, positioned upside down.

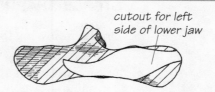

cutout for left side of lower jaw

The upside down chicken's right ilium with the cutout for the left half of the lower jaw, ready for marking up.

the hollow portion of the ilium faces toward the left, while the prominent ridge is to the right of the ventral process. (If it's the other way around you've got the ilium from the left side—swap them and start again.)

2: Find the cutout for the left side of the jaw. Hold the cutout in place so that its posterior edge lines up with the right-hand edge of the ilium. Press the anterior end of the cutout so that it contacts the hollow portion of the ilium. Adjust its position so that its lowermost edge lines up with the lowermost edge of the ilium. The anterior tip of the cutout will lie in the upper half of the hollow portion, as shown.

3: While holding the cutout in contact with the surface, trace around its outline using a sharp pencil. Remove the cutout and pencil over the outline.

Repeat steps 1–3 for the right side.

The chicken's left ilium, positioned upside down.

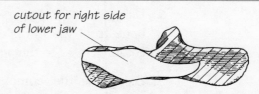

cutout for right side of lower jaw

The upside down chicken's left ilium with the cutout for the right half of the lower jaw, ready for marking up.

STEP 2: SHAPING THE SKULL AND LOWER JAWS

Do the following for each of the marked-up halves of the skull.

1: Starting with the most anterior perforation (the outline for the external naris), make a small hole right through the bone with one of the points of a small pair of scissors, using a rotating motion.

2: Once the hole is large enough for the needle file to penetrate, file out the perforation to the correct shape.

Repeat steps 1 and 2 for each of the other perforations. If you have a choice of files, you might want to experiment to see which one works best. I found a rounded file best for finishing off rounded portions, and a triangular one best for roughing out the perforations.

During the filing process it is possible that the outer layer of bone may flake away from the underlying bone, which is more porous. Such damage can be repaired by adding a small bead of glue to the damaged surface of the bone, replacing the flake, and pressing it gently into place. Any excess glue can be wiped off with your finger. Allow the bone to dry thoroughly for at least half an hour before continuing filing on that particular perforation.

Once all the perforations have been made, the edge of the bone has to be trimmed to the pencil lines. Start with the posterior end of the skull. This part of the bone is very porous and brittle, so great care is needed.

1: Using the nail clippers, chip off small (about 2 mm) pieces of bone from the lower corner of the ilium. Do not attempt to get any closer to the pencil line than about 2 mm.

2: Using the file, complete the shaping to the pencil line. To reduce the chances of splintering the bone, stroke the file in one direction, rather than using a back-and-forth action. Also, support the bony edge being filed between your finger and thumb.

The shaping of the rest of the skull has to be completed. Start with the anterior end of the skull.

1: Starting well in front of the line that marks the tip of the skull (at least 10 mm away), snip away with the nail clippers, along a line parallel to the pencil line. The chips you cut away will be fairly large (5–10 mm), giving a fairly jagged edge.

   Note: In the unlikely event that your ilium is so brittle that it starts shattering badly, stop using the nail clippers. Do all your shaping with the file. Large amounts of bone can be removed fairly rapidly, using the method described below under the heading "Hint."

2: Repeat step 2, trimming the edge of the bone progressively closer to the pencil line. Depending on how cleanly the bone snips away, and upon your confidence, you may want to continue until you are about 5 mm away from the pencil line. But if you are in any doubt, stop snipping—the rest of the bone can be safely trimmed away using the file, as explained below.

3: Using the nail clippers, snip away a number of small chips from the ventral process of the ilium. Continue until you are about 3 mm from the pencil line.

4: Complete the final shaping of the skull using the file. Be patient and careful, otherwise you may break the skull. If the edge you are filing looks fragile, support it with your finger and thumb.

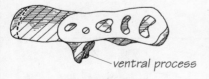

ventral process

The skull is shaped in stages, starting by snipping along an imaginary line, well in front of the final cut mark (shown by broken line). Once the rough shaping has been done, most of the ventral process is snipped away.

Filing is speeded up by notch-filing the bone and snipping off the resulting tabs.

If the skull should break, continue filing the bone down to the pencil line. The broken pieces can be glued together once the shaping is finished.

Hint: To remove large amounts of bone fairly rapidly, proceed in two stages. First, use a triangular file to make a series of deep notches, as shown. Then snip off the remaining tabs of bone with the nail clippers.

Once the shaping of the two halves of the skull is complete, the same has to be done for the lower jaws. Do this the same way, using the nail clippers to rough in the outline, then finishing it off with the file.

STEP 3: COMPLETING THE SKULL

The first job is to join the two halves of the skull together, and this requires a plasticine support.

1: Roll a piece of plasticine into a ball about 1 inch (2½ cm) in diameter. Flatten this into a rectangle, about 2 ½ inches (6 cm) long, 1½ inches (3 cm) wide and about ⅛ inch (5 mm) thick.

2: Press the pad of plasticine onto the top of a matchbox or similarly sized object.

The plasticine support for the skull, attached to the top of a box.

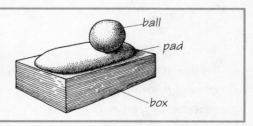

3: Make a ball of plasticine about ¾ inch (2 cm) in diameter and press this into one end of the plasticine pad, as shown.

The plasticine is used to support the two halves of the skull during the next stage of construction. Prop them up so that their posterior ends embrace the plasticine ball. Adjust the two halves of the skull so that:

1: The snout portion of each half is approximately vertical.

2: The dorsal margin of the snout region lies closer to the midline than the ventral margin (the **midline** is a line running down the center of the dorsal surface).

3: The two tips of the snout touch each other.

4: The posterior ends of the two halves make contact dorsally.

5: The ventral edge of the tip of the snout is about 7 mm lower than the ventral edge of the posterior end of the skull.

The two halves of the skull, propped up by the plasticine support.

Look at the skull from all aspects—from the front, back, top, and sides—making sure it is approximately symmetrical. When satisfied, apply a droplet of Krazy Glue to each of the contact points and allow it to set for about ten minutes.

You will find that the orbits of your skull (see the drawing on page 55) face backward rather than forward. Don't worry, this is an inescapable consequence of the curved shape of the chicken's ilia. It will not detract from the final appearance of the skull, and everyone will think the antorbital fenestra is the orbit anyway.

The next stage is to fill in the diamond-shaped gap in the skull roof. The anterior and posterior triangles of the diamond will be filled in with corresponding triangles cut from each of the two smallest ischia. Beginning with the posterior triangle, do the following.

1: Lay an ischium on the table with the broad end toward you and the narrow end pointing away from you. Run a finger over the broad surface. Does it feel slightly concave or mostly

WARNING ▼▼▼

Krazy Glue is toxic. It can cause serious damage if it comes into contact with your eyes, so safety glasses should be worn. Krazy Glue readily bonds with skin. It should not be used by youngsters.

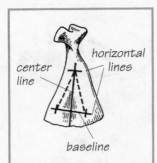

center line

horizontal lines

baseline

Marking up a chicken's ischium to fill the posterior triangular opening in the top of the skull.

convex? The concave surface needs to be uppermost, so if it is not, flip the bone over. Draw a vertical center line down the middle of the bone (it doesn't have to be *exactly* in the middle).

2: Measure the length of the posterior triangular opening in the skull roof. Transfer this length to the ischium using two horizontal lines, as shown. The lowermost line is the baseline.

3: Measure the width of the posterior triangular opening in the skull roof. Halve this width and measure this distance on either side of the center line, making small marks on the baseline. Complete the triangle by joining these marks to the intersection of the center line with the upper horizontal line.

4: Cut out the triangular area using the nail clippers and file, as before. Take a look at one of the cut edges. Notice that the bone comprises two sheets, joined together by a spongy filling. This is a strategy for increasing the strength of flat bones.

5: Check the fit of the triangular cutout with the corresponding opening in the skull roof, filing away more as necessary. When satisfied, run a thin bead of glue along the contact edges. Leave to dry for about one minute, then glue the bone in place.

Repeat steps 1–5 for the anterior triangular gap in the skull.

Once the skull roof has been completed and the glue has set, remove the skull from the plasticine support and turn it upside down. Consolidate the joins by running a bead of glue along their inside edges. Leave to dry for at least fifteen minutes.

The attachment of the skull to the vertebral support requires a small shelf of bone to be glued across the gap at the front of the upper jaw margins. Do the following:

1: Find the scapula on the skull plate. Measure off a 10-mm-long section from the straight outer portion of the blade, as shown in the drawing. Cut this piece out, using nail clippers (the dry bone should cut through cleanly without breaking).

Bone structure and strength

When you look at a broken bone you notice that the outer layer looks solid to the naked eye, whereas the inner portion looks spongy. The outer layer is called compact bone, while the porous layer is called cancellous bone. Compact bone is stiffer and stronger than cancellous bone, but it is much denser. If a bone were made of compact bone alone it would be very strong but also very heavy. Consequently, compact bone tends to be restricted to regions that have to withstand the largest forces. For example, the outer part of the shaft of long bones, like the femur, is compact bone, forming a tube. The two ends of the bone expand to form the joint surfaces, which articulate with other bones. Here the compact bone is much thinner, and is underlain by cancellous bone. The cancellous bone completely fills the space and transmits forces from the joint surfaces to the compact bone that forms the shaft. Most flat bones, like the ones forming the roof of our skull and our shoulder blades, are made of two sheets of compact bone joined together by a layer of cancellous bone. The same sort of construction is used in corrugated cardboard, where two flat sheets are joined together by a corrugated sheet. It is also used in the material called foam board, used for artwork, where a filling of styrofoam is sandwiched between two sheets of cardboard.

Cancellous bone appears spongy to the naked eye, whereas compact bone does not.

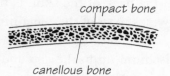

compact bone

canellous bone

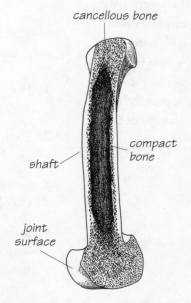

cancellous bone

shaft

compact bone

joint surface

CORRUGATED CARDBOARD

corrugated sheet

flat sheets

FOAM BOARD

plastic foam

cardboard

Corrugated cardboard (*top*) and foam board (*bottom*).

Cancellous bone is largely confined to the ends of long bones, while the shaft is formed largely of compact bone.

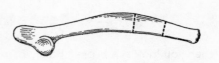

Marking up a chicken's scapula to make a plate for the inside of the upper jaw margins of the skull.

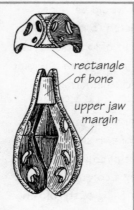

rectangle of bone

upper jaw margin

The anterior view (*top*) and ventral view (*bottom*) of the two halves of the jaw, showing the position of the rectangle of bone.

2: Test fit this rectangle of bone in the gap between the upper jaw margins at the front end of the snout. It will not be a good fit because the gap tapers toward the front. File the insert to the appropriate shape so that it fits inside the jaw margins, as shown in the diagram. Taper the edges of the bone, as well as the sides, to get a good flush fit (it should not be visible when the skull is viewed from the side).

3: Apply glue to the edges of the insert and the inside edges of the skull. Allow to dry for one minute, then secure into place. Run a thread of glue along the contact edges to consolidate the union.

The gap at the back of the skull is filled using a piece of bone cut from the widest part of the remaining ischium.

1: Hold the ischium up to the gap and check its fit. Mark off in pencil how deep the cutout needs to be, as shown.

2: Using the nail clippers, cut out the required segment of the ischium. As before, do not cut too close to the pencil line.

3: Complete the shaping of the cutout with a file, frequently checking it against the gap.

4: Measure the width of the lower edge of the cutout, and make a mark at the midpoint. Using a small, round file, make a notch at the halfway mark corresponding to the diameter of a wire coat hanger, as shown.

5: Glue the cutout in place. This will only close the lower part of the gap at the back of the skull—there will still be a gap above it.

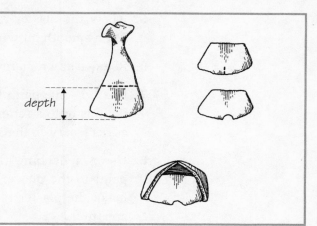

Marking up a chicken's ischium to fill the gap at the back of the skull (*top left*). Once the final shaping of the cutout is complete, the midpoint is marked in pencil (*top right*), and a round notch filed (*bottom right*). The cutout is glued in position, filling the lower part of the back of the skull (*bottom*).

All the remaining gaps in the skull will be filled with plaster. Proceed as follows.

1: Mix up a half teaspoon of Spackle, Polyfilla, or plaster of paris—it should be like thick toothpaste. Use a flat toothpick to apply the plaster where it is needed.

2: Fill in the dorsal gap between the two halves of the snout, as shown. Continue the plastering ventrally, filling in the gap between the lower parts of the two sides of the snout. This will complete the upper jaw margin in the front of the snout, as well as at the sides.

3: Fill in the gap at the back of the skull.

4: Fill in the gaps in the skull roof. Use the plaster sparingly, wiping off any excess so that it does not cover the surface of the bones. Save any leftover plaster.

Plastering in the gaps at the front of the snout (*left*) and at the back of the skull (*right*).

5: Allow the plaster to set for a couple of hours, or overnight. Then smooth off with a piece of fine sandpaper.

6: Remove any remaining pencil marks with an eraser.

7: Mix up some paint to match the color of the bone. Try painting this onto a scrap of leftover dried plaster. Adjust the color as necessary so that the painted plaster matches the bone.

8: Using a dabbing rather than a stroking action, apply the paint to the plaster in-filling on the skull. It is very easy to make the plaster blend into the bone so that it is no longer apparent.

▼▼▼ Step 4: Gluing the Two Halves of the Lower Jaw

1: Using the pad of plasticine, without the plasticine ball, set the two halves of the lower jaw together, as shown, so that:

   a. The tips touch.

   b. The distance between the posterior ends corresponds to that between the ventral edges of the posterior end of the skull.

   c. Each one is essentially vertical.

2: Remove one half of the jaw and file a small flat surface on the inside surface of the tip, where it contacts the other side. Return the jaw half to its original position.

3: Repeat step 2 for the other half of the jaw.

4: Make sure that the two halves of the jaw are still lined up correctly, and that their tips are touching. Add a small droplet of Krazy Glue to their tips, thereby cementing them together. Wait for a couple of minutes.

5: Check to see that the two halves are cemented together. This can be done by gently prodding one half of the jaw and seeing

Gluing the two halves of the lower jaw together.

if the other half moves in unison. If necessary, reglue. Once the two halves are joined, gently pry them free from the plasticine and turn them upside down. Consolidate the join with another bead of glue.

STEP 5: MAKING THE TEETH

Find the paper plate labeled *teeth*. It contains four fibulae, up to six small flat ribs, and six pubes. This will be more than enough to make the approximately sixty teeth that are required. These bones need to be bleached, so they are good and white. Proceed as follows:

1: Place the bones in bleach solution for fifteen minutes.

2: Boil the bones for about ten minutes. Remove the saucepan from the stove and flush with cold water, taking care not to lose the bones.

3: Remove one of the bones from the saucepan. Using the nail clippers, cut off and discard any part that is wider than 2 mm. Next, cut a series of teeth, as shown, so that each one has a sloping edge and a straight edge. Notice that this method involves no waste. The teeth need to be between 2 mm and 4 mm long. Use your artistic license to vary the length of the teeth.

    The small pieces of bone are liable to fly everywhere and get lost. There are two ways of preventing this:

a. Place a piece of dark cloth into a bowl and do all the snipping within the bowl. The pieces of bone will hit the cloth and show up against the dark background.

b. Do all the cutting inside a small plastic bag.

4: Repeat step 3 until all the bones in the saucepan have been cut up.

5: Spread the teeth out on a paper plate to dry overnight. Alternatively, spread them out onto a regular ceramic dinner plate.

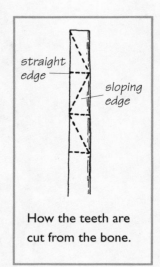

straight edge

sloping edge

How the teeth are cut from the bone.

Turn your oven on to a low heat for two or three minutes, then turn off the heat. Place the plate containing the teeth into the oven for five or ten minutes. This will thoroughly dry them out.

STEP 6: ATTACHING THE TEETH TO THE SKULL AND LOWER JAWS

1: Make a pad of plasticine about 2½ inches (6 cm) long, 1½ inches (3 cm) wide, and about ⅛ inch (5 mm) thick. Set the skull down on the pad, with its top facing down.

2: Run a bead of glue along the edge of the right side of the skull, from the snout back to the level of the middle of the antorbital fenestra (do not worry about the front of the snout, those teeth will be added later). Allow to dry for about thirty seconds.

3: Select the first tooth for the left side of the skull. Make sure the blunt end is square and not angled. If it looks angled, file it down square.

4: Hold the tooth in the forceps, as shown, so that it is ready for attaching to the skull, with the sloping edge facing toward the tip of the snout. Add a small bead of glue to the end of the tooth and allow it to dry for a few seconds. (This can be speeded up by blowing on the tooth.) Attach the tooth to the edge of the skull, close to the tip of the snout, and press it firmly into place.

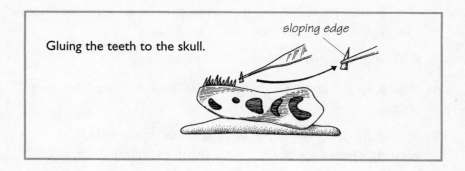

Gluing the teeth to the skull.

sloping edge

Tooth Replacement in Reptiles

We humans, being mammals, have two sets of teeth during our lives. When we are young we have a set of milk teeth, but these are replaced by another set when we get older. Reptiles, in contrast, constantly replace their teeth throughout life. Each new tooth forms at the base of an old one, and as it grows it starts pushing the old tooth out. Eventually the old tooth, which is large and often worn, is pushed out, leaving a small young tooth in its place. If several teeth were replaced at the same time in the same part of the jaw, this would cause an effective gap because of the small sizes of the replacement teeth. This undesirable situation is avoided by the way the teeth are replaced in a series of waves. The end result of these waves of replacement is that adjacent teeth are at different stages in their growth.

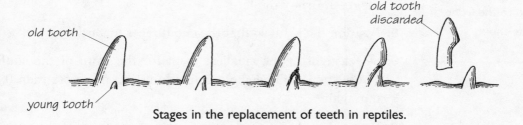

Stages in the replacement of teeth in reptiles.

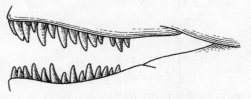

Reptilian teeth are replaced in a series of waves, to avoid large gaps.

5: Select the next tooth. Make sure that adjacent teeth are not the same size—a small tooth should be placed beside a large one. Repeat step 4, making sure that the teeth are touching, or almost touching, at their bases.

6: Continue until all twelve teeth have been attached to the right side of the skull. Select the teeth so that the last five become

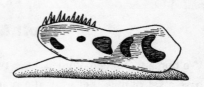

A complete set of teeth for one side of the skull. Notice the variation in length.

Gluing the small teeth to the front of the snout.

progressively smaller, though maintain some randomness in tooth size, as shown.

7: Make any last adjustments to the teeth. Using a toothpick, run a thread of glue along the inside edge of the right jaw margin, touching the inside edges of the teeth. This will keep the teeth firmly in place.

8: Position the skull so that the snout faces toward you.

9: Select eight of the smallest teeth for the front of the skull. These should all be about 2 mm long and not more than 0.5 mm wide.

10: Run a thread of glue along the edge of the front of the snout. Allow to dry for about thirty seconds, then attach the front teeth, one at a time, as you did before.

Repeat steps 2–9 for the other side of the skull.

Follow the same procedure for attaching the teeth to the two edges of the lower jaw as you did for the skull. Use twelve teeth for each half of the lower jaw. (There is not a row of small teeth in the front of the lower jaw as there is in the front of the snout.)

STEP 7: ATTACHING THE LOWER JAW TO THE SKULL

1: Modify the plasticine support used in step 3 on page 63 so that it will hold the lower jaw and skull in place, as shown. Experiment with the gape of the jaws until you have a realistic appearance. Make sure that:

a. The posterior ends of the jaw contact the back of the skull and extend about 2 mm further back.

b. The **mandibular symphysis** (the point of union of the two halves of the lower jaw, or mandible) is lined up with the middle of the snout.

2: When satisfied with the fit, use a toothpick strut to keep the correct gape, as shown in the illustration. This will keep the skull and mandible in the correct position during the gluing process.

3: Remove the skull and apply a smear of glue to each of the four points of contact between it and the mandible. While the glue is drying, place the skull with its roof flat down on the table.

4: Reposition the skull. Check to make sure that the mandible and skull are properly lined up again. When satisfied, consolidate the jaw joint by adding beads of glue, using a toothpick, to the inside surfaces of the skull and mandible.

5: Allow the glue to dry for five or ten minutes, then add more. You need to be generous with the glue, otherwise the jaw joint will be too weak. Allow to dry for at least thirty minutes.

Carefully remove the skull from the plasticine support. You will find that although the mandible is firmly attached to the skull, it is not rigid. This is because of the flexibility of the glue forming the jaw joint. If left like this, the mandible would gape

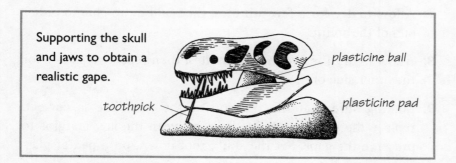

Supporting the skull and jaws to obtain a realistic gape.

plasticine ball

plasticine pad

toothpick

open when the skull was mounted on the skeleton. The jaw joint therefore has to be braced. Proceed as follows:

1: Using the X-Acto knife, trim part of a toothpick down to a thickness of about 0.5 mm. Cut off two splints, each about 7 mm long.

2: Modify the plasticine support so as to hold the skull horizontal, with one side facing toward you.

3: Using the forceps, place one of the splints in position on the inside of the furthest side of the skull. Adjust it so that it spans the gap between the skull and the mandible, about 5 mm anterior to the jaw joint. The splint should be approximately vertical, and each end should contact the inside surface of the skull, above, and the mandible, below.

4: Remove the splint and add beads of glue to the inside surfaces of the skull and mandible where they contacted the splint. Be generous with the glue.

5: Make a small (1 cm diameter) ball of plasticine and attach it to the table. Press the middle of the splint down into the ball so that the two ends are free. Liberally coat the exposed surfaces with glue and let dry for about 1 minute.

6: Using the forceps, remove the splint from its plasticine support and replace it, glue side down, into its original position. Press down its two ends so that they stick firmly to the skull and mandible.

7: Allow to dry for a few minutes, then add more glue to either end of the splint.

8: Allow to dry for five to ten minutes, then repeat steps 3–7 for the other side of the skull.

9: Making sure that the position of the mandible is correct, replace the small plasticine balls between the jaw margins to preserve the gape. Set the skull, roof down, on a pad of plasticine, and allow to set overnight.

You should now be the proud owner of a very realistic model of the skull of *Tyrannosaurus*.

Allison from Colorado, a keen model maker, wanted to add an extra touch of realism. By reference to the drawing on page 55, she scribed on the lines (sutures) that mark the joints between the individual bones of the skull and lower jaw. She then inked in the lines with a pen.

Your *T. rex* skull is anatomically quite accurate when viewed from the side. However, the mandibles are too narrow when viewed from the front, and the skull roof is diamond-shaped rather than triangular when viewed from above. These minor shortcomings are an unavoidable consequence of the limitations of the building materials provided by a chicken's skeleton. Keep the skull safe—I used an old 35-mm color slides box.

▼▼▼ Building the Vertebral Column

Before choosing the vertebrae for your dinosaur you need to learn how they fit together. To find out, take a look at *How the Vertebrae Fit Together*.

Find the plate labeled *vertebrae*. There are four strings labeled *thoracic vertebrae* and four strings labeled *sacral vertebrae*. In addition, there is a short string labeled *sacral vertebrae* and some fused sacral vertebrae labeled *partial sacrum*. There are also two furculae and two radii—bones that will be used to make the small vertebrae at the end of the tail.

STEP 1: COLLECTING AND MODIFYING YOUR DINOSAUR'S NECK VERTEBRAE

Tyrannosaurus has ten cervical vertebrae, but the first one, the atlas, is very small and would not be visible in the mounted skeleton. Consequently, we are only going to use nine cervicals. *Tyrannosaurus* has a short neck, with relatively small vertebrae, which will be modeled from the chicken's sacrum. Before starting, you need a 4-inch (10 cm) length of coat hanger for tem-

How the Vertebrae Fit Together

thoracic vertebrae

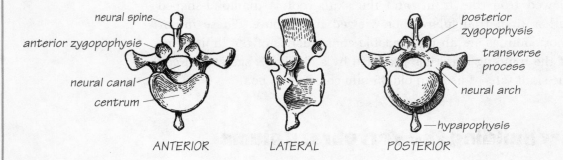

neural spine

anterior zygopophysis

neural canal

centrum

ANTERIOR

LATERAL

posterior zygopophysis

transverse process

neural arch

hypapophysis

POSTERIOR

Details of the vertebrae. The bottom illustration of two vertebrae, seen from above, shows how the zygapophyses fit together.

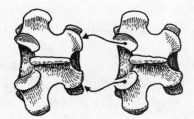

Pick up one of the three strings of thoracic vertebrae from the vertebrae plate. Hold it with the anterior end in your left hand and posterior end in your right hand.

Notice how the plastic twist tie passes through the neural canal. The bone that arches to form the canal is called the neural arch. Below the neural arch is the main body of the verte-bra, the centrum. If you look at the centrum from the back (or from the front), you'll see that it has a double curvature, being curved from side to side as well as from top to bottom. This saddle-shaped surface (termed *heterocoelic*) is unique to birds.

Keeping the vertebrae still loosely strung on the plastic twist tie, try fitting two vertebrae together so that the saddle-shaped articular surfaces meet. Notice how snugly they fit. Pull the vertebrae apart again. Remember that the anterior (head end) of the vertebral column is toward the left, the posterior end to the right.

Look closely at the posterior end of the vertebra that is in your right hand. On either side of the neural arch, just above the neural canal, is a small round disk, called a **zygapophysis**. Each disk faces down and out. Push the vertebrae together again. Notice how the posterior zygapophyses meet a similar pair on the anterior end of the other vertebra. Can you see which way the latter disks, the anterior zygapophyses, face? They face up and in. If you look down on the tops of the vertebrae as you articulate and separate them, you'll get a good view of the way the zygapophyses fit together. Their function is to help keep the vertebrae in line and to stabilize the vertebral column, while allowing movement. If you remember that the posterior zygapophyses, like bad gamblers, are always down and out (while the anterior ones face up and in) you'll always get the vertebra the right way around. While looking down on the thoracic vertebrae, notice the large processes that point laterally. These are the transverse processes, and they form part of the attachment for the ribs. Try holding up a forked rib to one of the thoracic vertebrae, making sure you choose a rib from the appropriate side. The shortest branch of the fork (the tuberculum) articulates with the transverse process, while the long branch (the capitulum) fits into a round depression on the side of the centrum, close to the centrum's anterior edge.

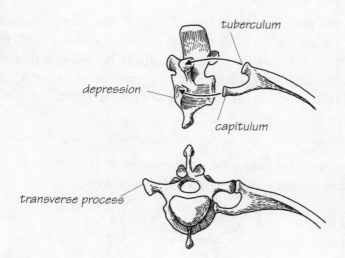

How the two branches of the rib articulate with the vertebra. Shown from the left side (*top*), and from the front.

porarily retaining your dinosaur's cervical series. You can use the top loop of your coat hanger, first straightening it out. Alternatively, snip off the required length from the straight section of a second coat hanger. Attach a short strip of masking tape to one end of this rod, pinching the two ends together. This will stop the vertebrae from slipping off. Proceed as follows:

1: Pick up one of the four long strings of separated sacral vertebrae. If there is any difference in their sizes, choose the string with the smallest vertebrae. Notice that the most posterior ones, probably three or four, have stout transverse processes which are double. You need four of these for the start of the cervical series. Remove four from the sacral string. If you do not have enough on one of the sacral strings, take what you need from one of the other sacral strings. Arrange them in order of increasing size, with the smallest one to your left.

2: Starting with the smallest vertebra, file each end of the centrum so that it is flat, taking care not to damage the transverse process. Continue filing a little off each surface until the centrum is 3 mm thick (anterior to posterior).

3: Using the nail clippers, snip off one of the transverse processes (either one). File the stump more or less flush with the centrum, but do not file too much, otherwise you will damage the fragile centrum. The remaining transverse process will become the neural spine of your first neck vertebra.

Modifying a chicken's posterior sacral vertebra, to make it an anterior cervical vertebra of the dinosaur.

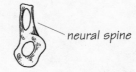

transverse process   neural spine

4: Try threading the centrum onto the rod. The end of the rod with the masking tape is designated anterior, so thread the vertebra on so that its *neural spine* slopes back.

Chances are that the hole in the vertebra (the neural canal), is too small. If so, widen the hole using the pointed end of the small round file. If you are careful you'll be able to widen the smallest vertebra until it fits. Don't worry if it breaks, it can easily be repaired with glue.

Threading the anterior cervical vertebrae onto the rod. Seen from the left side.

5: Repeat steps 2–4 for the next largest sacral vertebra. This time remove the transverse process corresponding to the one you removed previously. To check which one you need to keep, slip the vertebra onto the rod, transverse process sloping back (away from the masking tape end of the rod). Line it up with the other vertebra, and see which of the two transverse processes matches up with that of the first vertebra. Also, when filing down the centrum, do this obliquely so that the ventral width is slightly less than the dorsal width. Making the centrum slightly wedged in shape gives the neural spine more of a backward rake.

6: Repeat step 5 for the remaining two sacrals.

Find the string labeled *partial sacrum*. Look at the fused series of five chicken sacrals. The most anterior ones have fairly prominent rectangular neural spines. They decrease in size posteriorly. They will be flipped around so that the fifth one, the most posterior, becomes the most anterior one. Slip these vertebrae onto the rod so that the smallest one leads. Check how well it matches up with the last (largest) of the free cervicals on the rod. The neural spine of the last (most posterior) of the free cervicals is longer than that of the first of the fused ones. However, the centrum of the first fused vertebra is much larger than that of the last free one. Tilt the first fused vertebra upward so that the ventral surface of its centrum is level with, or a little higher than, that of the last of the free cervicals. Notice that there is now very little difference in the apparent heights of their neural spines.

first neural spine

last centrum

Modifying the chicken's fused sacral series, to make it the dinosaur's posterior cervical vertebrae. Seen from the left side.

You may be able to get a better transition by changing the order of the last two or three of the free cervicals. You could also file a small amount from the tip of the neural spine of the last free cervical vertebra. When satisfied with the gradation (it won't be perfect!) do the following:

1: Remove the fused chicken sacral series. Using an X-Acto knife (or scalpel), shave a small amount from the anterior and posterior edges of the first neural spine. Do the same for the anterior edge of the second neural spine, thereby making a gap between them. Angle the blade while paring, to give a raked-back appearance to the neural spine, as shown.

2: Repeat step 1 for the succeeding neural spines, but this time use a small flat file, if you have one, or an emery board.

3: File the posterior surface of the last (largest) centrum flat. Continue filing until the centrum is 4 mm thick (anterior to posterior). The quickest way to do this is by rubbing it on a piece of medium sandpaper.

4: Take a pipe cleaner and twist a short length of plastic twist tie around one end to stop the vertebrae slipping off. This is designated the anterior end. Thread the nine cervical vertebrae onto the pipe cleaner in the correct sequence, with the smallest one closest to the twist tie. Make sure they go on the right way around, with their neural spines raked back. Wrap a piece of twist tie around the pipe cleaner to mark the end of the neck vertebrae.

At this stage you've got all nine cervical vertebrae and must now select the thirteen dorsals and five sacrals. Remember, the dorsal vertebrae of a dinosaur (or other reptile) are those that lie between the last neck vertebra and the first sacral one. In humans and other mammals, these are referred to as the thoracic and lumbar vertebrae.

STEP 2: COLLECTING AND MODIFYING THE DORSAL AND SACRAL VERTEBRAE

The dorsal vertebrae need to be only 5 mm thick (anterior to posterior), so each one will have to shaved down. This is best done by rubbing the vertebra on a sheet of sandpaper. This will reduce, or remove, the zygapophyses, but that does not matter. The neural spines will have to be made narrower, too, and some will have to be shortened—use a file or emery board for this. Your objective is to produce a series of dorsal vertebrae that grade gently in size. Although they are all about the same size, they tend to be smaller at the beginning, where they grade into the cervical vertebrae. Proceed as follows.

1: Look at the strings of vertebrae labeled *thoracic vertebrae*. Is each set about the same size as the others? If there are any obvious size differences, rearrange the strings so that the top string has the smallest vertebrae and the bottom string has the largest ones. Place each string so that the most anterior vertebra is to the right. Untie the posterior end of the twist tie of each string. You will select vertebrae from this posterior end.

2: Choose the smallest vertebra and slip it off its twist tie. Slip it onto the pipe cleaner with the cervical vertebrae. Make sure that the anterior end of this vertebra faces toward the anterior end of the pipe cleaner. How does this vertebra, the first dorsal, match up in size with the last cervical vertebra?

The first dorsal should not be smaller than the last cervical—ideally it should be a little bigger. If it is too small, choose a larger one.

3: Having made a satisfactory size match between the last cervical and first dorsal vertebra, the latter can be modified. First, file a flat face on the anterior and posterior ends, using sandpaper. Take about the same amount from each end and continue until the centrum is 5 mm thick (anterior to posterior). Next, reduce the anterior-to-posterior width of the neural spine, filing it down so as to give it a slightly backward rake,

Modifying a chicken's thoracic vertebra to become the dinosaur's first dorsal vertebra. Seen from the left side. The scale measures 5 mm.

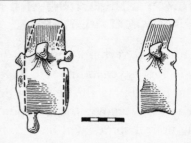

as shown. Lastly, file off the small knob of bone beneath the centrum (called the **hypapophysis**, found on most of the thoracic vertebrae).

Repeat steps 2 and 3, selecting progressively more anterior vertebrae from the vertebral strings until you have all thirteen dorsals. Note that the last three dorsals should be filed to a centrum thickness of 6 mm rather than 5 mm. Ideally, the dinosaur's dorsal vertebrae should increase in size slightly, up to about number 7, and then remain the same size. There should be a steady increase in the widths of the neural spines throughout the series, and a slight increase in their heights, as shown.

Note: It is possible that one or two of the vertebrae you

The dinosaur's complete set of dorsal vertebrae, seen from the left side.

The dinosaur's complete set of sacral vertebrae, seen from the left side.

selected have posterior zygapophyses that extend well beyond the level of the posterior surface of the centrum (this is true of the first two of the chicken's back vertebrae). In this event, simply file the protruding processes down until they are in line with the centrum.

Having completed the cervical and dorsal vertebrae, tie a piece of twist tie around the end of the pipe cleaner to stop the vertebrae from slipping off. Attach a label to the other end that reads *cervical and dorsal vertebrae*. Place onto a new paper plate labeled *finished vertebrae*.

Select five more vertebrae, for the sacrum. These will be largely hidden from view by the pelvis, so don't use your five largest remaining vertebrae—save them for the first part of the tail. Trim each centrum down, as before, but to a thickness of 6 mm. File each neural spine so that it is approximately the same size as the neural spine of the last dorsal vertebra. Thread these five vertebrae onto a second pipe cleaner, making a loop at either end to stop them from slipping off. Attach a label at the anterior end of the series that reads *sacral vertebrae*. Put them on the plate with the finished dorsal vertebrae.

STEP 3: COLLECTING AND MODIFYING THE CAUDAL VERTEBRAE

The number of tail vertebrae in *Tyrannosaurus* is not known for sure. A rough count made in the field while collecting the most complete skeleton ("Sue") indicated thirty-six or thirty-seven. This may be on the low side—the last few tail vertebrae are quite small and easily lost. We will err on the generous side and take forty-five as the number. The first caudal vertebrae will be selected from the vertebrae remaining on the vertebral strings; the others will be manufactured from the other bones on the vertebrae plate.

Procedure:

1: Take a pipe cleaner and twist a small length of plastic twist tie around one end, which will be the anterior.

2: Look carefully at the remaining sacral vertebrae. Some, the most anterior ones, have an obvious neural spine. There could be as many as sixteen of these. Arrange them in order of decreasing size. Select the last fourteen vertebrae, discarding the larger ones. Do not worry if there are fewer than fourteen.

3: Check the thickness (anterior to posterior) of each centrum. If any exceed 6 mm, file them down to this size.

4: Thread the vertebrae onto the pipe cleaner, in decreasing size order. Make sure that the anterior end of each one faces toward the twist tie. It is often difficult to distinguish anterior from posterior because the zygapophyses are so small, but there is an easy way. If you look at the vertebra from the side you will see a small notch at about the level of the transverse process. This notch is posterior in position. If you should find that the vertebra you have just added looks larger than the previous one, swap them around. The important thing is that the vertebrae appear to decrease gradually in size.

5: File each neural spine down, making a gap of 2–3 mm between adjacent ones. Remove equal amounts of bone from the anterior and posterior edges. The neural spines should be vertical or slightly raked back—they must not be raked forward. No neural spine should be taller than that of the vertebra in front. At this point you will have up to fourteen vertebrae on your pipe cleaner.

The differences in shape in the chicken's sacral vertebrae. The ones at far right are discarded.

6: Attach a label to the anterior end of the pipe cleaner that reads *caudals 1–22*. You need to select the remaining vertebrae to complete this string of 22 caudals.

Examine the remaining sacral vertebra. Some have long transverse processes that are single. Others have long processes that are double. Still others have hardly any transverse processes at all. The latter have huge neural canals, reducing the vertebra to a ring of bone. Discard these vertebrae. Do the following:

1: Snip off the single processes, as close to the centrum as possible. Use the small plastic bag to catch the pieces—they will be used later as chevron bones (a **chevron** is a small bone attached beneath the centrum, like an inverted neural spine).
Label the bag *chevrons* and add them to the *finished vertebrae* plate. File any remaining stubs flush with the centrum.

2: Repeat step 1 for the vertebrae with the double process, snipping through one branch at a time. Each double process will probably separate into two pieces as it is cut. If not, snip them apart, saving them in the plastic bag. You will be leaving an intact double process as your dinosaur's neural spine.

3: Lay all of the processed sacral vertebrae flat on the table. There could be as many as twenty-five of these, though there could be considerably fewer. You need a total of twenty-two vertebrae for the labeled pipe cleaner. Subtract the number you already have from twenty-two—you will need eight or more.

4: Select the required number from the processed sacrals. They should decrease in size—the largest one should match up in size with the last vertebra (most posterior) on the pipe cleaner. Thread these vertebrae, in order of decreasing size, onto the pipe cleaner, and tie them off with a length of twist tie. Add this to the finished vertebrae plate. Chevron bones have to be added to some of the vertebrae, but this will not be done until the skeleton has been mounted.

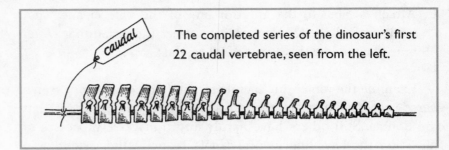

The completed series of the dinosaur's first 22 caudal vertebrae, seen from the left.

The remaining twenty-three caudal vertebrae have to be manufactured from the furculae (wishbones) and radii remaining on the vertebrae plate. Proceed as follows:

1: Put the two furculae and two radii into a saucepan of hot water, bring to a boil, and simmer for no less than thirty minutes. Turn off the heat and add cold water to the saucepan to cool its contents.

2: Remove one of the furculae from the water. Using nail clippers, snip off and discard the thick end of one of the two branches. Cut a series of short rods, some 3 mm and others 4 mm long. If necessary you can use a small plastic bag to stop the pieces from flying everywhere. Do the same for the other branch, discarding the thick central portion.

3: Repeat step 2 for the other furcula.

4: Remove one of the radii. Using an X-Acto knife, cut off 10 mm from either end and discard them. If you use firm pressure and a rocking (not sawing) action, it will cut without shattering. Cut the rest into 5-mm lengths. Make sure to cut squarely across the bone so that the ends are not angled. You should get about six or seven pieces. Retain them and any pieces less than 5 mm that are left over.

5: Repeat step 4 for the other radius, but cut into 4-mm lengths.

6: Take a piece of plastic twist tie, 20 cm long, and strip off the plastic covering to expose the wire. Make a loop at one end.

7: Arrange the cut sections of bone in decreasing order of size, based on both length and depth. Line them up so that their anterior and posterior ends touch. Measure the combined length of the pieces. Also measure the combined lengths of caudal vertebrae 1–22. The total length of these two sections should be 23 cm.

If the total length of the tail exceeds 23 cm, the excess will be taken out of the cut sections of bone, not from the first twenty-two caudals. In this event do the following:

1: Check the lengths of the individual segments of bone. The longest ones (those cut from the radii) should not exceed 5 mm. Shorten any that are too long, using the file.

2: Check that half of the sections cut from the radii are 4 mm rather than 5 mm long. Rectify any discrepancy.

3: Repeat steps 1 and 2 for the segments cut from the furculae, making sure that the measurements here are 3 and 4 mm.

4: Rearrange the cut sections end-to-end and remeasure. If still too long, simply delete some of the sections, choosing one of each length, as far as possible.

(In the unlikely event that the total length of the tail is less than 23 cm, add some more cut segments, using bones taken from the spare parts plate.)

Once you have a satisfactory series of bone sections, start threading them onto the wire, commencing with the largest one.

The completed series of the dinosaur's last 23 caudal vertebrae, seen from the left.

Check each one for cracks—these often run the entire length of the section. Smear a bead of glue along the crack, thereby sealing it. You may have difficulty threading some of the smaller segments onto the wire. If so, soak them in water for a minute or so and try again. When all the bones have been strung on, wrap a small piece of tape around the wire to retain them. Add a label to the anterior end that reads *caudals 23–45,* and add to the finished vertebrae plate. Any leftover sections can be added to the spare parts plate. Check to make sure you have everything on your finished vertebrae plate.

CONTENTS OF FINISHED VERTEBRAE PLATE

Four strings of vertebrae, labeled as follows:

1. *cervical and dorsal vertebrae.* A twist tie separates the cervicals from the dorsals.
2. *sacral vertebrae.* The anterior end is marked by a label and the pipe cleaner is twisted into a loop at each end.
3. *caudals 1–22.*
4. *caudals 23–45.*

A plastic bag labeled *chevrons.*

▼▼▼ Building the Hind Legs

You will find all the bones needed for making the hind legs on the plate labeled *hind legs and feet.* This contains one pair of femora, one pair of ulnae, two pairs of radii, and one pair of hand bones (major metacarpals). It also contains the bones for making the feet—dealt with in a later section.

STEP 1: MARKING UP THE BONES

The bones have to be boiled prior to cutting in order to soften them, so all the cut marks and labels have to be penciled heavily onto the bone. Groups of bones will be kept together by placing them into plastic sandwich bags, suitably labeled. They will be kept inside the bags during the boiling, too. The first bone to be marked up is the femur. (Note: We'll mark arrows on the bones to show which direction is up.)

The Femur

Find the pair of femora. Each femur has to be shortened by removing a section from the middle of the shaft. This makes the proportions of the femur more like those of a *Tyrannosaurus*. However, it also removes the curvature of the shaft, a feature birds share with theropod dinosaurs.

Do the following for each femur:

1: Look at the two ends of the bone. Notice how porous they are. This shows that the chicken was immature and that the ends were capped with cartilage—you probably remember removing it during the cleaning process. The bones of some hatchling dinosaurs have a similar appearance, for similar reasons. One end of the femur has a pair of **condyles** (a double knob). This is the lower, or knee, end of the bone. If you look carefully, you'll see that one of these condyles is slightly shorter

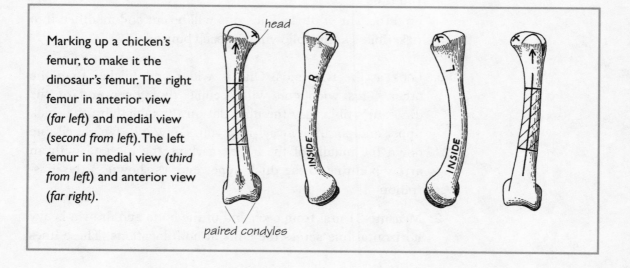

Marking up a chicken's femur, to make it the dinosaur's femur. The right femur in anterior view (*far left*) and medial view (*second from left*). The left femur in medial view (*third from left*) and anterior view (*far right*).

head

paired condyles

and thicker than the other. This shorter condyle is on the inside of the femur. Look at the upper end of the femur. When viewed end-on this appears triangular, with a condyle, the **head of the femur**, on the inner side. Mark the head of the femur with an X. Mark the femur with a letter R for right or L for left. (Even if you'd lost the labels saying which side they were, you could easily work it out for yourself. You know that the head of the femur, which you've marked with an X, is at the top of the bone, and is on the inside—that is, it faces toward the hip.) Write *inside* on the inside edge of the femur.

2: Lay the femur down, with the upper end pointing away from you, so that the two condyles rest on the table. The shaft of the bone will curve toward you, away from the table (you'll find this is the only position in which the femur will lie still). You are looking at the front surface of the femur. Draw a heavy, vertical pencil line down the middle of the front surface, with an arrow pointing toward the top end of the bone. Measure 23 mm from each end of the bone and draw a heavy line, horizontally, across the bone at both locations. These lines are cut marks. Label each bone *fm* for femur and L or R for left or right. Put them both into a plastic bag and label it *femora*.

The tibia

Find the pair of ulnae. Each one will be cut and modified into a single tibia. Do the following for each bone.

1: Look at the two ends. One is wider and thicker than the other. This wide end will become the upper end of the dinosaur's tibia. Lay the ulna flat on the table with the thick upper end pointing away from you. Draw a heavy pencil line down the middle of the bone, marking the top end with an arrow pointing to the thick upper end, as shown in the illustration.

2: Measure 21 mm from each end of the bone and draw a heavy horizontal line across the bone at both locations. These lines

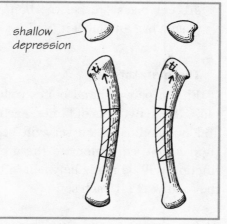

Marking up a pair of chicken's ulnae, which will become a pair of dinosaur's tibiae. The shape of the top end of each bone is shown at the top. Notice the shallow depression, which will be referred to again on page 96 when the tibia and fibula are glued up.

shallow depression

are cut marks. (You may have some problem deciding how to make this measurement, because the top end of the bone is angled to the shaft—simply measure to the top of the angled end).

3: Label each bone *ti* for tibia. Put them both into a plastic bag and label it *tibiae*.

The fibula

Find a pair of radii. Each radius will become a dinosaur's fibula. Do the following for each one:

1: Look at the two ends. One is wide and flat, while the other is rounded. The flattened end will become the upper end of the dinosaur's fibula. The shaft of the bone is curved. Lay the bone on the table so that the shaft arches toward you. Draw a heavy pencil line down the middle of the shaft—this will be the outside of the fibula (you may find it easiest to use the edge of the pencil lead). Mark the top of this line with an arrow pointing to the flattened end of the bone.

2: Measure 21 mm from each end of the bone and draw a heavy horizontal line across the bone at both locations. These lines

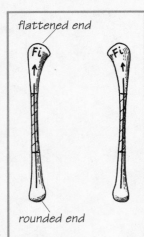

flattened end

Fi

rounded end

Marking up a pair of chicken's radii, which will become a pair of the dinosaur's fibulae.

are cut marks. Label the bone *fi* for fibula. Put them into a plastic bag and label it *fibulae*.

The metatarsus

Find a pair of hand bones (major metacarpals) and a pair of radii. Make two sets of bones, each set comprising one hand bone and one radius. Each set will become a dinosaur's metatarsus (upper foot, equivalent to the arched part of our foot). No distinction will be made between left and right for these bones. Do the following for each set:

1: Look at the hand bone. This will become the inner metatarsal bone. One end, which is a little narrower, is thick and squarish, while the other is more flattened. The thick end will become the upper end of the dinosaur's inner metatarsal.

2: Lay the hand bone down with the thick end pointing away from you. Mark the upper end of the shaft with an arrow pointing toward the thick end. Measure down 24 mm from this thick end and draw a heavy horizontal line across the shaft. This is a cut mark. Label the bone *m* for metatarsal and *I* for inner.

3: Look at the radius. As before, notice that one end is flattened while the other end is rounded. The flattened end will become the lower end of the dinosaur's middle metatarsal.

4: Lay the radius down with the flattened end pointing toward you. Draw an arrow pointing away from this flattened end, as shown in the illustration. Measure 24 mm up from this flattened end and draw a thick horizontal line across the shaft. This is a cut mark. Label the bone *m* for metatarsus and *M* for middle (make sure the label is below the cut mark). The other end of the bone will become the top end of the dinosaur's outer metatarsus.

5: Draw an arrow pointing toward the rounded end of the radius. Measure 24 mm from this end and draw a thick hori-

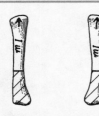

Marking up a pair of chicken's hand bones, which will become a pair of the dinosaur's inner metatarsal bones.

zontal line across the shaft. This is a cut mark. Label this end of the bone (above the cut mark) *m* for metatarsal and *O* for outer.

Place both sets of marked-up bones into a plastic bag marked *metatarsi.*

STEP 2: CUTTING THE LIMB BONES

Note: As an alternative to boiling and cutting the leg bones with nail clippers, you can use a small hacksaw and cut through the dry bones. The advantage of this method is that you can get a good clean cut without any shattering, and you don't have to pre-boil the bones.

Boil some water in a saucepan. Meanwhile, add about half a cupful of hot water from the tap to each of the plastic bags containing bones to be cut. Tie each bag with a plastic twist tie. There are four bags altogether, labeled *femora, tibiae, fibulae,* and *metatarsi.* When the water comes to a boil, place the plastic bags into the saucepan. As each bag goes into the saucepan, stab it several times with a knife. This will let the air out and the hot water in. Let the bones boil for fifteen minutes.

Remove the bags and cool them under a cold tap. Allow the bags to drain for a few minutes. **Important: put the bag containing the metatarsals to one side—they have their own special cutting procedure**. Do the following for the other bones:

1: Remove the bones and the label. Dab the bones dry with tissue and put them onto a paper plate, with their label. Using the nail clippers, cut squarely across the penciled cut marks.

Take care not cut at an angle, because this will make it difficult to join the cut ends together afterward. Discard the center pieces you cut from each bone.

Don't worry if the bones do not cut cleanly, because they can be filed down later. Save any broken pieces—you may be able to put them back in place right away, while the bone is still soft and damp.

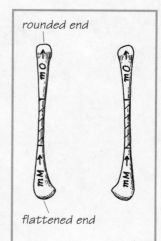

rounded end

flattened end

Marking up a pair of chicken's radii. The lower end of each one will become the dinosaur's middle metatarsal bone, while the upper end will become the outer metatarsal bone.

2: Leave the bones to dry thoroughly before gluing. There are two ways of doing this. You can either do this within about a half hour by using a table lamp, or you can leave them overnight to air-dry. To use the fast method, simply adjust the lamp so that it shines horizontally, then place the bones on the inside of the shade. Alternatively, you can put the bones directly onto the bulb. Provided it is no brighter than 60 watts, it will not scorch the bones until several minutes have passed, but keep an eye on them.

You'll probably find that boiling the bones has made the pencil marks much fainter. If this is the case, pencil over the marks again when the bones have dried.

Procedure for the metatarsi

Using nail clippers to cut through these bones often causes shattering. To avoid this, use the X-Acto knife. Start by placing the bone to be cut onto an old newspaper. Position the blade on the cut mark and press down firmly, using a rocking action (**not** a sawing action). Jagged edges can be filed down later. Divide into two sets, each set comprising an outer, inner, and middle metatarsal. Leave to dry.

STEP 3: GLUING THE HIND LIMB BONES

Paleontologists use large boxes filled with sand to hold bones in a vertical position while the glue is setting. You can do the same by filling some empty cans with sand. This is the best method, but as an alternative, you can use a strip of plasticine instead. Stick a strip of plasticine about 4 inches (10 cm) long, 1½ inches (4 cm) wide, and ½ inch (1 cm) thick onto the tabletop. After you have glued bones together, press them vertically into the plasticine and leave them to set. If you decide to use the plasticine method, read "plasticine strip" for "sandbox" in the sections that follow.

The methods for gluing the leg bones of your dinosaur are

similar to those used for mending full-size dinosaur bones. Follow these instructions for each of the leg bones to be glued—these are the femur, tibia, and fibula. (The metatarsus is treated separately.)

1: Test fit the two halves by bringing their cut ends together. Make sure that the pencil line is on the same side for each half, and that it lines up fairly closely. File off any jagged edges with the nail file.

2: The largest bones, the femur and tibia, need some internal supports, namely a small piece of toothpick. Break off a piece of toothpick about three-quarters the length of the bone to be joined. Sharpen both ends with the X-Acto knife. Push one end of the toothpick halfway into one of the cut ends, making sure it goes in straight. Hold the other half of the bone in line with the first half, so that its cut end is about 1 mm from the free end of the toothpick. Now push the two ends of bone together, so that the toothpick penetrates the second half of bone.

The two halves of the bone should fit together properly and be in line. If they are not in line, pull them apart and try pushing them together again. If they are still not lined up properly, you can try removing the toothpick and start over again. If you still don't have any luck you can try enlarging the hole for the toothpick, using an intact toothpick.

Pull the two halves of the bone slightly apart—just enough to squeeze in some glue. Apply the glue to both ends of the bone and allow it to dry for a about thirty seconds. Then push the pieces of bone firmly together.

3: Stick one end of the glued bone into the sandbox so that it stands up. Make sure that the bone has a label beside it. Let the glue dry for about an hour. The fibula doesn't need the toothpick treatment. Simply add a drop of glue to each cut end, let it dry for about a minute, then push the two ends together.

STEP 4: FILLING IN THE CRACKS IN THE GLUED LEG BONES

Because the fit between the ends of the bones that you glued will not be perfect, there will be some gaps across the joins. There may also be some broken edges that will need filling. Make these repairs in the following way.

1: Mix up one level teaspoonful of Spackle, Polyfilla, or plaster of paris with a few drops of cold water in a paper cup to make a thick paste.

2: Using the wide end of a flat toothpick, apply some of the plaster to the gaps in each of the leg bones. Push the plaster deep into the cracks. It doesn't matter if there is a ridge of extra plaster around the crack, because this will be removed later— but try not to smother the bone in plaster! Take particular care not to cover over any of the penciled labels. Wait for ten minutes, then wipe off the excess plaster with a tissue.

3: Leave the plaster to dry for about fifteen minutes. If it doesn't feel dry at the end of this time, leave it until it does. Add a few drops of water to one end of a Q-Tip and squeeze dry. Using the damp tip, wipe off the dried plaster from the surface of the bones—but avoid wiping the actual cracks.

This is a convenient time to glue the tibia and fibula together. Do the following for each pair of bones:

1: Look at the top end of the tibia. Viewed from the top, the bone is triangular, with a shallow depression on its shortest edge, as shown in the drawing on page 91. This depression is on the outer edge of the tibia, the side to which the fibula attaches.

2: Hold the tibia and fibula side by side with their top and bottom ends in contact. Make sure that the shaft of the fibula bows away from that of the tibia, as illustrated. Also, make sure that the top end of the fibula rests against the shallow depression.

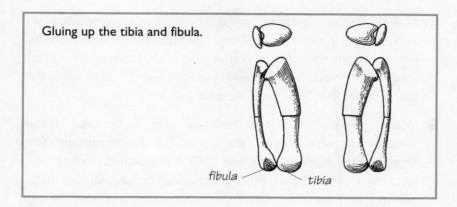

Gluing up the tibia and fibula.

fibula — tibia

Lastly, make sure that the bottoms of the two bones are flush. Do this by holding them against a flat surface. Their tops may not be flush like their bottoms, but that's all right.

3: Separate the bones and apply a dab of glue to their points of contact. Allow the glue to dry for about a minute, then press them together again. Apply additional beads of glue to consolidate the union.

Draw a line down the middle of a paper plate. Put the left femur on one side of the line, together with a glued tibia and fibula. Put the right femur on the other side with the other glued tibia and fibula. Label the plate *finished legs and feet,* noting which is left and right.

The last major step in building the hind legs involves the metatarsal bones.

STEP 5: ASSEMBLING THE METATARSAL BONES

Do the following for the first set of three metatarsal bones:

1: Find the middle metatarsus (mM). File down the broad end so that it is symmetrical and reduced in width to 4 mm.

2: Carefully file down any jagged edges from the cut ends of all three bones.

Filing down the broad end of a dinosaur's middle metatarsal bone (*left*) so that it becomes symmetrical (*right*).

3: Make a disk of plasticine, about 1¼ inches (3 cm) in diameter and ¼ inch (6 mm) thick. Press the three bones into the plasticine so that they are in contact, with their arrows pointing away from you. The arrows point toward the top of the metatarsus, that is, toward the ankle.

4: While pressing the top ends of the outer and inner metatarsals together, push the top end of the middle one further into the plasticine so that it slips beneath the other two, as shown in the illustration. The middle metatarsal should be about 1 mm lower than the other two. The width of the top end of the metatarsus should not be more than 12 mm. The width of the bottom end should not exceed 14 mm. If necessary, you can file a little bone from the lower ends of the three metatarsals.

5: Repeat steps 1–4 for the other set of metatarsal bones, but reverse the order of the outer and middle ones. For example, if the inner metatarsal was on the left side in the first assembly, place it on the right side in this one.

6: When satisfied with the arrangement of each set of metatarsal bones, they can be glued. Apply small droplets of Krazy Glue, or regular cement, to the points of contact of the individual bones.

7: Allow thirty minutes setting time for the regular glue. If using Krazy Glue, you can check to see if the bones are glued within a few minutes. Check by gently moving one of the bones to

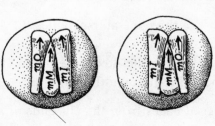

plasticine disk

Assembling the metatarsal bones on their plasticine disks. Those on the left represent the dinosaur's right upper foot, the other set representing the left side.

see if the others move too. If necessary, add more glue and leave to set again.

8: When the bones are set, remove from the pad and clean off any adhering plasticine. Strengthen the joints with additional glue, added to both sides.

For simplicity, I'll call each set of glued metatarsal bones the **upper foot**. Allow the glue to harden for about two hours, then do the following for each upper foot.

1: Look at the back surface (the one opposite the penciled arrows). The top end of the middle metatarsal bone projects well beyond the level of the other two. Trim this down until it is flush with the others. Use a file, sandpaper, or an X-Acto knife. This will expose the hollow marrow cavity of the bone. Clean out any brown material (dried blood).

2: Mix up a small quantity of Spackle or Polyfilla and fill the opening at the top of the middle metatarsal bone. Also seal the cut lower ends of all three bones. Allow to set for at least an hour. If necessary, smooth off with fine sandpaper.

3: Distinguish between left and right upper feet. Lay one of them on the table so that you can see the arrows. The anterior surface faces you. Is the inner metatarsus (mI) on your left or right? If it is on your left it is the LEFT upper foot.

4: Make two balls of plasticine, each about 1½ inches (4 cm) in diameter. Flatten each into a disk about 2¼ inches (6 cm) in diameter and about ¾ inch (2 cm) thick. Make two more balls about ¾ inch (2 cm) in diameter. Shape each one into a low cone and attach it to its own disk, close to one edge, as shown in the illustration.

5: Find the left upper foot and press it up against the plasticine cone, about 4 mm above the disk, with its anterior surface facing away from the cone. Lean the upper foot back slightly, as illustrated. Using a pencil, scribe a bold letter *L* on the side of the disk.

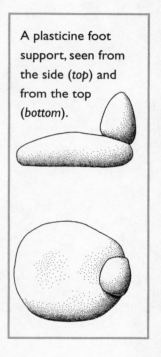

A plasticine foot support, seen from the side (*top*) and from the top (*bottom*).

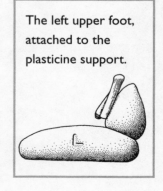

The left upper foot, attached to the plasticine support.

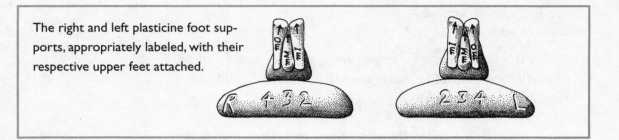

The right and left plasticine foot supports, appropriately labeled, with their respective upper feet attached.

6: Turn the disk around so that the anterior surface of the upper foot faces you. The metatarsal bone on the left is the inner one; the one on the right is the outer one. The inner metatarsal supports the inner toe, which is actually the dinosaur's second toe (see the box called *Toes and Feet*). Scribe *2* on the left side of the edge of the disk, as shown in the illustration. The outer metatarsal bone, on the far right, supports the dinosaur's outer toe, which is its fourth. Scribe *4* on the right side. The middle metatarsal supports the dinosaur's third toe, so scribe *3* between the 2 and 4.

Repeat steps 5 and 6 for the right upper foot.

This completes gluing the metatarsals. Assembling the dinosaur's feet, which is the next job, will be done on the plasticine supports you built for them.

▼▼▼ Building the Hind Feet

STEP 1: CUTTING THE TOE BONES

Find the plate labeled *hind legs and feet*. It contains six forked sternal bones. These will be used for making the toe bones that form the feet. The toe bones will be cut from the longest fork of each sternal bone, as shown in the illustration. Usually, they can be cut without having to be boiled first, so you can assemble the toe bones into feet right away. However, if the bones start shat-

Toes and Feet

A theropod's three metatarsal bones are elongate, and extend the length of the lower part of the leg. Each metatarsus supports one toe, which is directed forward. These three correspond to toes number 2, 3, and 4. The first toe, which corresponds with our big toe, is attached at the back of the innermost metatarsus, about halfway down. It points backward and is therefore called the reversed hallux. In birds that perch in trees, the reversed hallux is used for gripping the branch.

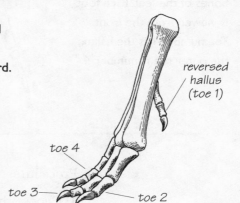

reversed hallus (toe 1)

toe 4

toe 3

toe 2

tering when you cut them, boil them first. Then allow them to dry for at least an hour before assembly. Both feet will be built at the same time. As the toe bones are snipped from the sternal bones, simply press them into place on the plasticine supports, as shown in the illustration. Use nail clippers, and do the snipping using a cloth-lined bowl, or a plastic bag, to prevent losing bones. **Note:** Each of the toe bones of the first row—those that lie in contact with the metatarsal bones—will be cut from the ends of the six sternal bones. The slightly dilated ends of these bones will be placed in contact with the metatarsal bones.

IMPORTANT:

1. Be very PRECISE in your measurements—check the length of each toe bone before adding it to the foot, correcting any errors in length.
2. Cut each bone SQUARELY.
3. Every toe bone must be pressed TIGHTLY against the next bone in line, otherwise the foot will not glue properly.

cut marks

A chicken's forked sternal bone, showing how it is used for cutting out the dinosaur's toe bones.

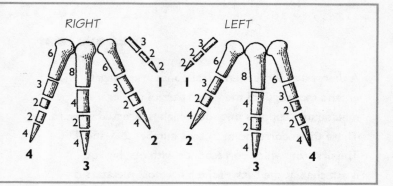

The lengths of the individual bones of the feet. Each foot is viewed from the front. Toe number 1 is the hallux; the outer toe is number 4.

Procedure:

1: Choose the two largest sternal bones, based on the width at the end of the longest fork. Measure 8 mm from this end, mark with a pencil, and cut off squarely. Use these two bones for the middle toe of each foot. Press the bones into the plasticine just enough to keep them in place. If you embed them, it will be difficult to remove the foot once it is glued.

2: Cut 6-mm lengths from the ends of each of the remaining sternal bones. Use these four bones as the outer and inner toes of each foot.

This completes the first row of toe bones for both feet. Make sure that this row is inclined slightly with respect to the metatarsals, as shown in the illustration of the side view of the foot. They should be inclined at about 45 degrees to the horizontal.

By reference to the diagram that gives the lengths of each toe bone, complete the feet, up to the level of the terminal claws. Notice that toe bones from row two on are set at an angle to those in the first row, as illustrated in the side view of the foot. They should be inclined at only a few degrees to the horizontal. If there is any variation in the widths of the toe bones, use the widest ones for the uppermost rows. Also, try to make the middle toe the stoutest.

Note: Put the discarded portions of the sternal bones onto the spare parts plate for later use.

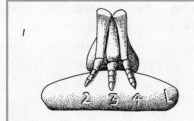
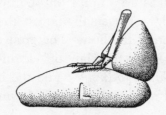

The left foot, except for the hallux, shown from the front (*left*) and from the outside (*right*).

The Terminal Claws

Each of the dinosaur's toes ends in a sharp claw; these are made from the fibula bone. Do the following for each (dry) fibula:

1: Using the nail clippers, snip off the last 25 or 30 mm, so that the part you keep is at least 1 mm wide at its cut end. Save the end piece for later use.

2: Hold the upper end of the fibula so that the cut end rests against the tip of your finger. Using this finger as a support, file an angle on one edge, as shown in the illustration.

3: File a second angle on the opposite edge, thereby making a wedge-shaped point. (Don't try to make a rounded point by filing all the way around the tip—this doesn't work because the bone is hollow).

Filing one of the two angled edges on the tip of the fibula. The finger is used to support the bone while it is being filed.

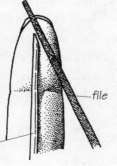

fibula supported by finger

file

Filing a notch across the fibula in preparation for breaking it, using a flat file (*top*) and a triangular file (*bottom*).

4: Measure 5 mm from the tip, making a pencil mark. Place the edge of a small file on the mark and file a narrow groove across the bone. The groove weakens the bone, allowing you to snap the claw off cleanly. (See the box *How Cracks Cause Things to Break*.) File the broken edge off squarely. Keep on filing until the claw is 4 mm long.

Repeat steps 2–4. You should be able to get three or four claws from each fibula.

The claws become thicker toward the top end of the fibula, so you will have a range of thicknesses. Select the best fit for your dinosaur's toes.

STEP 2: GLUING THE TOE BONES

1: Taking great care not to get Krazy Glue on you, gently squeeze a droplet of the liquid from the end of its nozzle and touch it against each bone joint. The idea is to get the liquid to run into the crack between the two contact edges of the bones (by capillary action). Krazy Glue will not bridge a gap, and will therefore join two bones together only if they are in contact. Do not worry if the Krazy Glue leaks over the surface of the two bones being joined. However, you do not want it running onto the plasticine, where it will solidify as an extension of the toes, so go sparingly. When satisfied that all the joints have been glued, proceed to the next step.

2: Using a toothpick, apply a thread of clear glue across the fronts of the top ends of the metatarsal bones, to consolidate the joints. You can also use some clear cement to consolidate any of the other joints that may look in need of attention. However, go very sparingly with the cement, and only apply it to the joint surfaces. Leave the feet for several hours for the cement to set.

3: After the glue has set, carefully begin removing each foot from the plasticine. This is best done by undercutting each toe with an X-Acto knife and gently prodding and coaxing it free.

How Cracks Cause Things to Break

Cracks weaken structures. This is because the material in the immediate vicinity of a crack is unable to transmit any of the stresses acting on the structure. Consequently, a greater burden is placed on the adjacent material, and this concentration of stress tends to extend the crack further. We use this mechanism of stress concentration to break things in our everyday lives, as when we make a small scissor cut in a piece of material before ripping it in two. This also explains the grooves in chocolate bars and the perforations in toilet rolls.

Some years ago there was a terrible crash of a DC–10 airliner, caused when one of the engine pylons failed during takeoff. The pylon attaches the engine to the wing, and when it broke, the engine, which was under full thrust, tore away, causing such extensive damage to the wing that the aircraft flipped over. An investigation revealed that maintenance crews had been using the wrong procedures when replacing engines on the DC–10. This placed excessive stresses on the engine pylon, causing small cracks to appear on the surface. These cracks went unnoticed until one of them led to a catastrophic failure.

This led to a grounding of all DC–10 aircraft while inspections were made of their engine pylons. Defective pylons were replaced and correct maintenance procedures were instigated so that the problem would not be repeated. Since then there have been no more problems, and this very fine aircraft has enjoyed an excellent safety record.

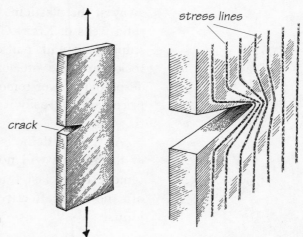

When a crack appears in a piece of material under stress (*left*) it is weakened, because of the concentration of stresses (*right*).

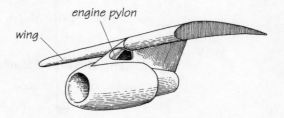

Cracks in the engine pylon, which suspends the engine from the wing, caused catastrophic failures.

Be patient, and the foot will eventually come free. If any of the bones come loose, they can be reglued by placing them into contact with one another and touching them with a small droplet of Krazy Glue.

You now have to remove the excess plasticine and do some additional gluing. Do the following for each foot.

1: Lay the foot on crumpled tissue with the underside facing upward. Hold the upper bones to steady the foot and pare away at the plasticine with an X-Acto knife. If there are any solid webs of Krazy Glue attached to the bones, they can be snipped off with nail clippers. I had some extensive webs of rock-hard glue on some of the toes of my dinosaur, and despaired of ever removing it. However, I was pleasantly surprised at how easily it snipped off, without any damage to the tiny bones.

As the plasticine is white, and since it is on the underside of the foot, it will not show. Therefore, you don't have to remove every last trace. However, the more you can clean off, the more effectively you will be able to consolidate the joints.

2: Using a toothpick, and with the underside toward you, apply small beads of clear cement to any of the joints that are not already well glued. Even if none of the joints need attention, run a thread of glue between the ends of the upper bones, as you did on the other side. Put the finished feet on a plate and label it *finished legs and feet*.

The Reversed Hallux: An Optional Extra

As already noted, *Tyrannosaurus* and its theropod relatives have a reversed "big toe" or hallux, the same as in birds. It is much reduced in size, though, and is attached to the posterior surface of the inside metatarsal bone, about halfway up. It is so small that it can be omitted from your skeleton without any great loss. However, it is easy to make. Find the two terminal pieces of fibula left over from making the claws for the feet, and do the following to each one:

Assembling the three bones that form the hallux on a ball of plasticine. Seen in side view

1: Measure the width of the bone at its tip. Use nail clippers to snip off anything that is less than 0.5 mm wide. Supporting the tip with a finger, file it to a point (the bone is solid here so you can make a round point). Measure 2 mm from the tip and snip off squarely (avoid using a pencil mark, as this will be difficult to remove later).

2: Measure off another 2 mm and snip off.

3: Measure off 3 mm and snip off.

4: Assemble the three segments, in the same order, on a piece of plasticine, giving them a slight curvature, as illustrated.

5: Glue up the joints using Krazy Glue, as for the other toes. Allow to set for about ten minutes, then remove from the plasticine.

No distinction is made between the left hallux and the right. They will be attached to the rest of the skeleton during the final stages of its assembly, so put them on the finished legs and feet plate.

▼▼▼ Building the Pelvis

Find the paper plate labeled *pelvis*. It contains one pair of ilia, one pair of ischia, and one pair of forked sternal bones.

Tyrannosaurus, as mentioned earlier, is a saurischian or lizard-hipped dinosaur, and has a three-pronged pelvis. The upper prong is the ilium; below it is the pubis (in front) and the ischium (behind). You'll build the dinosaur's pelvis in two halves, starting with the left side.

You'll use the chicken's ilium for the dinosaur's ilium, but it will have to be trimmed down in length. This is because birds have longer ilia than their theropod relatives. The dinosaur's pubis will be made from the chicken's ischium, while its ischium will be made from a part of the chicken's sternum. This part of the sternum is not joined to the rest until the bird reaches maturity. As noted earlier, it is referred to here as the forked sternal bone.

All of the bones have to be marked up prior to shaping.

STEP 1: MARKING UP THE PELVIC BONES

You will use cutouts for marking the outlines onto two of the three bones, as when you built the skull. Find the page with these cutouts and carefully cut around the outlines of the left and right ilium and the left and right pubis. Put these cutouts onto the plate labeled *pelvis,* and do the following:

1: Find the left ilium. Lay it down flat on the table, so that the external surface faces toward you. (As noted earlier, it will not lie flat if placed the other way up.) The front of the ilium, with its anterior hollow, lies toward the left. (If it's the other way around you've got the ilium from the right side—swap them and start again.) Notice the short prong that points downward—this is the ventral process.

2: Lay the cutout for the left ilium on the outside surface of the bone and line it up so that:

a. The most posterior of the three ventral processes of the cutout is positioned centrally over the ventral process of the chicken's ilium.

The paired cutouts for the dinosaur's ilia, positioned on the chicken's ilia, ready for marking up.

cutout

LEFT   RIGHT

overhanging middle
ventral process of cutout

posterior process of cutout

ventral process of
chickens' ilium

b. The dorsal edge of the cutout is level with that of the ilium, from about the level of the bony ventral process to about the level of the anterior notch in the cutout.

The middle ventral process will probably extend below the ventral edge of the ilium, but that is all right. However, make sure that the anterior ventral process of the cutout does not extend beyond the ventral edge of the ilium.

3: Taking care not to move the cutout, draw its outline on the bone. Remove the cutout and pencil over the outline with a strong line. Label the bone *il* for ilium, and *L* for left.

4: Look at the ilium from the posterior end. Notice that the ventral process is hollowed, and that this hollow is elongated in the direction of its most ventral point. Draw a cut line across the hollow, so as to cut off the most ventral point. This line should be parallel to the pencil line marking the posterior edge of the dinosaur's ilium. Hold the ilium by the ventral process, between your finger and thumb, with the ball of your thumb fitting snugly inside the elongated hollow. The cut mark follows the line of your thumbnail. Continue the line all the way around the ventral process, following along the edge of your finger.

Repeat steps 1–4 for the right ilium.

Before marking the outline of the dinosaur's pubis on the chicken's ischium, it is necessary to distinguish certain of its fea-

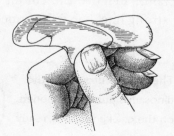

Holding a chicken's left ilium by the ventral process, ready to mark it up for cutting. The outline of the dinosaur's ilium has already been penciled in.

tures. Look at one of the bones. Notice that there is a flat triangular blade, and a narrow part that branches into two short prongs. One of the prongs is round and the other is flat. The flat prong is easy to hold between your finger and thumb. This flat prong will eventually be cut off. Draw a bold pencil line all around the base of the flat prong to mark the cut line. Repeat this for the other ischium. For simplicity, we will not distinguish between the chicken's left and right ischia. However, the distinction is made between the two sides for the dinosaur's pubes.

Start by marking the outline for the left pubis:

1: Lay one of the chicken's ischia on the table with the flat prong against the surface. Lay the cutout for the left pubis over the bone. The fit will not be perfect because the edge of the fan of the ischium is not an exact match for the curvature of the **boot** of the pubis. *Boot* is the name usually given to the large bony process at the end of the pubis—I prefer the term *pubic peduncle,* but this is not often used.

Line the cutout up so that:

a. The lowermost edge of the boot of the pubis follows along the edge of the fan of the ischium.

b. The top end of the pubis is centered on the rounded prong of the ischium.

c. The narrow shaft of the pubis is approximately in the middle of the ischium.

2: Taking care not to move the cutout, draw its outline on the bone. Remove the cutout and pencil over the outline with a strong line. Label the bone *pub* for pubis, and *L* for left.

The paired cutouts for the dinosaur's pubes, positioned on the chicken's ischia, ready for marking up.

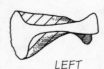

LEFT   RIGHT

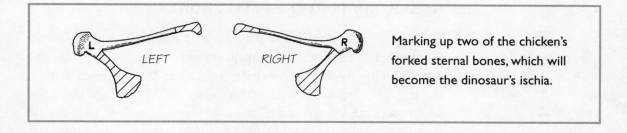

Marking up two of the chicken's forked sternal bones, which will become the dinosaur's ischia.

Repeat steps 1–2 for the chicken's other ischium.

Marking up the chicken's bones for the dinosaur's ischia does not require a cutout. However, it is necessary to determine left from right:

1: Pick up one of the forked sternal bones. Look at the region where the two branches meet. The surface is flat on one side, but the other side has something of a ridge.

2: Lay the two bones on the table so that the flat surfaces are uppermost and the long branches are horizontal and face away from you. The bone whose short branch faces toward the left will be the dinosaur's right ischium, the other the left.

3: Draw a straight line across the top of each short branch, at the point where it joins the long one, as shown. This is a cut line, and the short branch will be discarded. Distinguish between left and right with the appropriate capital letter, written above the line.

4: Measure 40 mm along the long branch from the thick end of the bone and mark a cut line across the bone.

5: Label each of the two bones *is* for ischium.

Now that the three pelvic bones for each side have been marked up, they are ready for final shaping.

STEP 2: SHAPING THE PELVIC BONES

Each bone is trimmed down to its pencil lines using the same techniques as used when building the skull. Use the nail clippers for removing most of the excess bone from the posterior end of the ilia. Clippers are also used for snipping through the cut lines on the ischia. All the rest of the trimming is done with a file. If you go carefully you will be able to avoid breaking the bones. In the event of a mishap, finish doing all the shaping in the vicinity of the break, including filing down any pieces that broke off, prior to making repairs.

STEP 3: GLUING THE PELVIS

Each half of the pelvis will be glued separately. However, to ensure that left and right sides are as close as possible to being mirror images, they will be built at the same time. Do the following for each half of the pelvis:

1: Make a plasticine ball about 1½ inches (4 cm) in diameter and shape it into a blunt cone. Make a plasticine roll about 1 inch (25 mm) long and ¼ inch (6 mm) in diameter and meld this along one top edge of the cone, as shown.

2: Lay the ilium down on the cone with its dorsal edge propped by the roll of plasticine. Press the roll firmly against the edge of the ilium to give it support. Adjust the ilium so that it lies parallel with the table; that is, so that it is horizontal.

3: Position the pubis and ischium as illustrated, making sure that the two bones are touching each another and that the ischium contacts the ilium. Use the file, where appropriate, to improve the area of contact between the bones.

4: Depress the **distal** (farthest from the body) ends of the pubis and ischium so that they lie about ⅝ inch (15 mm) below the level of the ilium. Make the angle between the ischium and pubis about 90 degrees.

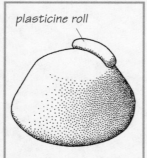

plasticine roll

Completing the support for one side of the dinosaur's pelvis by adding a roll to the blunt cone of plasticine.

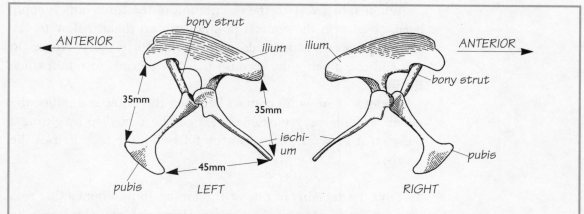

Assembling the three bones of each side of the dinosaur's pelvis, shown in side view. The bony strut is added later. Sample measurements are shown, in millimeters, for guidance.

5: Adjust the pubis so that the boot lies parallel with the table. Check the spacing and positioning of the three bones by placing your eye on the same level and inspecting them from all angles.

To give you some idea of the relative positions of the three bones, some point-to-point measurements are given in the drawing. These are only to serve as a guide—you do not have to try to match them exactly. What is important, though, is that your own point-to-point measurements are the same for both sides of the pelvis. Check them frequently.

The distal ends of the pubis and ischium are depressed below the level of the ilium. The bony strut is added later.

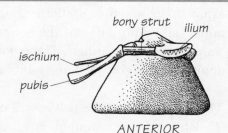

When satisfied with the orientation of the three bones, apply beads of glue to the contact points between them. Allow to dry for a few minutes, then add more beads if necessary. **Note:** Do not add too much glue, because the pelvis needs to retain some flexibility.

Because there is no contact between the ilium and pubis, the pelvic girdle is very unstable. This can be remedied by gluing a bony strut between them. Do the following for each half of the pelvis:

1: Find the remains of one of the forked sternal bones that was used for making the toe bones. Using the nail clippers, snip off the narrowest branch at the point where it joins the short, wide one. Discard the latter. Position the bone in the gap between the ilium and pubis, with its widest point touching the ilium. Mark off the length required to bridge the gap with a pencil mark. Be generous with the measurement—it is better to make the strut too long than too short, because it can be filed to the correct length after cutting.

2: Snip through the pencil mark with the nail clippers. Check the length of the strut against the gap, making any necessary adjustments with a file. The fit can be improved by filing a flat facet at either end of the strut, corresponding to its area of contact with the ilium and pubis.

3: When satisfied with the fit, add glue to all the points of contact. Wait about thirty seconds, then press the strut into place.

4: Check to see if the bones are glued. Do this by using an X-Acto knife to loosen the plasticine at the points of contact with bone. Gently prod one of the bones to see if the movement is transmitted to the others. If the bones are not properly glued, apply beads of glue to all the joints and leave to set.

The two halves of the pelvis will not be joined together until the skeleton is being mounted. Put them on the pelvis plate.

▼▼▼ Building the Pectoral Girdle

The pectoral girdle comprises two bones on either side of the body: the scapula, or shoulder blade, and the coracoid, which doesn't have a common name. The two bones are fused together as a single unit in *Tyrannosaurus,* the scapulocoracoid. Each one will be made from the remnants of the sternal bones, used earlier for making the toe bones. The outlines of each will be traced onto the bones using cutouts.

STEP 1: MARKING THE OUTLINES

1: Find the remnants of the forked sternal bones on the spare parts plate, used in making the feet. Have a look at one of the bones in the region where the two branches meet. As noted earlier, one side is flat, while the other has a slight ridge. With this in mind, choose two bones that form a pair. Lay them down with the flat surfaces facing upward, and the branch that has been cut (the narrower of the two) facing toward you. Which way does the cut branch point? If it points toward the right, mark it with an *R*. This will become the right scapulocoracoid. The other cut branch faces left. Mark that bone *L,* to become the left scapulocoracoid, as shown in the drawing.

2: Locate the remains of the cutouts page. Find the illustrations for the left and right scapulocoracoids and cut them out.

Marking up the remnants of two of the chicken's forked sternal bones. These will become the dinosaur's paired scapulocoracoids.

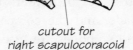

cutout for
right scapulocoracoid

cutout for
left scapulocoracoid

The paired cutouts for the dinosaur's scapulocoracoids, positioned
on the chicken's forked sternal bones, ready for marking up.

3: Place the cutout for the right scapulocoracoid on the corresponding forked sternal bone and line it up as shown in the
illustration. Trace around the outline with a sharp pencil.

Repeat step 3 for the left side.

STEP 2: SHAPING THE PECTORAL GIRDLE

Do the following for each one of the marked-up scapulocoracoids:

1: Use nail clippers to snip off the remnants of the cut branch.

2: File the edges of the bone down to the pencil line.

3: Reduce the thickness of the narrow end of the bone to about 2
mm, using a file.

Draw a line down the center of the pectoral girdle and limbs
plate, labeling the two halves *left* and *right*. Put the two shoulder
girdles into the appropriate halves.

▼▼▼ Building the Forelimbs

One of the most remarkable features of *Tyrannosaurus* is the smallness of its front limbs compared with the rest of the body. Furthermore, the hand is reduced to two fingers, each ending in a sharp claw (there is a remnant of a third digit, but it is too small to be modeled). The forelimbs will be built from bones found on the spare parts plate. The humerus, radius, and ulna are built from sternal ribs, while the hand is made from a fibula.

The finger bones will be snipped off, assembled, and glued in the same way the feet were built. However, the bones for the arms have to be boiled prior to cutting, then left to dry before gluing.

STEP 1: MODELING THE ARM BONES

1: Find a small pair of sternal ribs. These should be about 15–20 mm long, and about 2 mm thick. These will become the humeri. Measure 14 mm from the widest end and make a pencil mark across the shaft. Drop both bones into a saucepan of hot water.

2: Find some really small ribs whose thickness is 1 mm or less. You need four 7-mm lengths of this thickness. Make cut marks on the bones accordingly and drop them into the saucepan.

3: Bring the water to boil and simmer for ten minutes. Run cold tap water into the saucepan to cool the contents.

4: Remove the bones from the water. Dab dry on tissue, then cut as indicated. Leave the bones to dry for about two hours. Alternatively, use the fast drying method (page 94).

5: Draw two 1½-inch (4 cm) circles on a small piece of paper, labeling them *humerus* and *radius and ulna*. Put it onto the pectoral girdle and limbs plate, adding the limb bones to the appropriate circle.

Marking up a small pair of sternal ribs, to become the dinosaur's humeri.

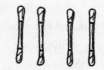

Marking up four really small chicken ribs, which will become the dinosaur's paired ulnae and paired radii.

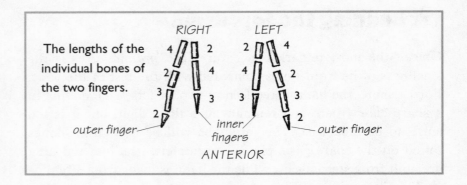

The lengths of the individual bones of the two fingers.

RIGHT   LEFT

outer finger — inner fingers — outer finger

ANTERIOR

STEP 2: BUILDING THE HANDS

As shown in the diagram, the two fingers have bones of different lengths. The four bones of the longest (outer) finger are each only 1 mm thick. The three bones of the shortest finger are just under 1 mm thick. Both hands will be built at the same time. Proceed as follows:

1: Make two plasticine disks, each about 1½ inches (4 cm) in diameter and ¼ inch (6 mm) thick. Mark one *L,* for left, the other *R.* Make two plasticine balls, each ½ inch (1 cm) in diameter. Attach one to the center of each disk.

2: Take two fibulae from the spare parts plate. Using the diagram as a guide, snip off segments of fibula of the appropriate size, and assemble the two hands. Attach each finger bone to the surface of the plasticine balls, as shown in the illustration. Make sure there is touch contact between all the bones in a given finger, and between the first bones of each finger.

3: When satisfied, glue the bones together with Krazy Glue, using the same technique as before (page 104). Be especially careful not to use too much glue, because an extensive cleanup job will be difficult on such a small hand.

Leave the hands to set for about twenty minutes. Meanwhile, check to see whether the bones on the pectoral girdle and limbs plate are dry. When they are, and when the hands have set, carry on with the next step.

Assembling the bones of the right hand, shown from the front (*left*) and outside (*right*). (Plasticine disc not shown.)

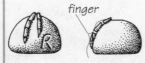

finger

STEP 3: COMPLETING THE FORELIMBS

Do the following for each hand:

1: Lay a radius and ulna, side by side, on top of the plasticine ball, as shown in the drawing. Make sure the bones touch the two fingers and each other.

2: Make a small plasticine ball, ¼ inch (6 mm) in diameter. Attach this to the back of the other plasticine ball, behind the radius and ulna. It will serve to support the humerus.

3: Position the humerus behind the radius and ulna with its cut end contacting them, as shown.

4: Make sure all the appropriate bones are in contact and correctly positioned, then secure the joints with Krazy Glue.

5: Allow about thirty minutes for the glue to set, then carefully remove the limb from the plasticine support. You can try carving the adherent plasticine from the fingers using the tip of an X-Acto knife blade. You can leave a thin ridge of plasticine at the back of the fingers—it won't show and it will reduce the risk of damaging the fingers.

Adding the radius and ulna to the hand. Same views as before.

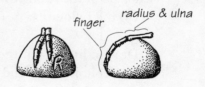

Completing the forelimb by adding the humerus. A second ball of plasticine has been added to support the humerus.

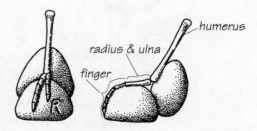

6: Distinguish between left and right arms—the shortest finger is on the inside (the thumb side). Place each arm on the appropriate side of the pectoral girdle and limb plate.

▼▼▼ Preparing the Ribs

Your dinosaur needs thirteen pairs of ribs. They are shortest at the front, rapidly increase in length up to the sixth pair, which is the longest, and then decrease again. You should have enough ribs for the job—six pairs from each chicken—but they are often so badly broken that many of them are unusable. Chickens have fairly short ribs, too, and many of them will need extending by adding sections from other ribs. You'll therefore find that ribs tend to be in short supply. The first job is to sort the ribs and see what you have.

STEP 1: SORTING THE RIBS

The ribs should already have been sorted into left and right, but it will be useful to refresh your memory on how to do this. Just lay a rib down with the shortest branch of the fork touching the table, and the forked end pointing away from you. Does the concave side of the rib face left or right? If it faces left it's a left rib.
Do the following:

1: Draw a line down the middle of a sheet of paper, heading the two columns *left* and *right*. Arrange the ribs on the paper in order of increasing size. (Most of the ribs will be about the same size.)

2: Draw a line down the center of a paper plate labeled *finished ribs*. Mark one side *left,* the other *right,* and mark the top of the plate *anterior ribs*.

3: Starting at the top of the size-ordered ribs, choose the smallest pair and place them at the top of the plate. These will be your dinosaur's first pair of ribs. Repeat, but this time place the next-smallest pair at the bottom of the plate, to become the dinosaur's last pair of ribs.

Repeat step 3 until you have thirteen pairs of ribs on the plate. The largest ones will be in the middle, diminishing in size toward the top and bottom. Save the leftover ribs; they will be needed in the next part.

STEP 2: MODIFYING THE RIBS

Ribs 5, 6, 7, and 8 have to be extended in length, and ribs 11, 12, and 13 have to be made shorter, according to the chart below:

Rib Number	Length
5	45 mm (1¹³⁄₁₆ inches)
6	50 mm (2 inches)
7	45 mm (1¹³⁄₁₆ inches)
8	45 mm (1¹³⁄₁₆ inches)
11	25 mm (1 inch)
12	20 mm (¹³⁄₁₆ inch)
13	15 mm (⅝ inch)

Do the following for each one of the four pairs of ribs that have to be extended, returning them to their proper place afterward:

1: Remove the rib from the plate and look at the end opposite to the fork—the lower end. Notice how the last 4 mm or so swells into a rounded ending. Using nail clippers, cut off the last 4 mm. Cut squarely across the shaft. The rib should cut through cleanly without shattering, so it is not necessary to boil it first. If necessary, file the end straight.

2: Find a similarly sized leftover rib. Line it up with the shaft of the rib just cut, as shown in the drawing. Slide the second rib down the shaft of the first until the distance between its lower end and the forked end of the first rib is the desired

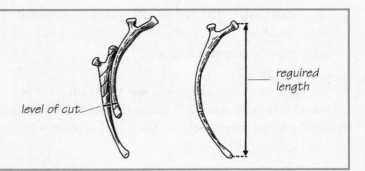

Lining up a second rib alongside the first. The lower end of the second rib will be used for extending the length of the first rib to the required length.

level of cut

required length

length according to the table. Mark the shaft of the leftover rib to show where it needs to be cut.

3: Cut the end off the leftover rib, at the pencil mark, and glue it to the end of the other rib. Allow the glue to set for one hour, then rub down the join with a file to remove any unevenness. If necessary, fill in any gaps with plaster. Allow to set for another hour, then rub down with sandpaper.

4: Shorten the relevant ribs by snipping the required amount from their ends, making sure to do this squarely.

5: Return all ribs to the finished ribs plate, arranging them in pairs in their correct order, left and right ones on either side of the line.

At this point you have all the parts ready for the final mounting of the skeleton. But there are a few small things to be done with them first.

▼▼▼ Last-Minute Preparations

STEP 1: CLEANING ALL THE BONES

Clean all bones of any remaining pencil marks by rubbing with a file or sandpaper, or by scraping with an X-Acto knife. In removing left/right labels, be sure to replace the unit onto a properly labeled paper plate, so that its correct identity is not lost.

STEP 2: TOUCH-UP PAINTING

Check all parts to see if any touch-up painting is required. Some patches of plaster may have been missed. Some bones may be badly discolored compared to those close by.

▼▼▼ Making the Wooden Base and Metal Supports

STEP 1: MAKING THE WOODEN BASE

Your piece of wood for the base should be about 20 inches (50 cm) long, 5 inches (13 cm) wide, and preferably at least ¾ inch (2 cm) thick. As noted earlier, some hardware stores sell finished pieces of wood of the appropriate size, described as "craft board." A length of wooden molding of the appropriate width works well too. For an added touch, you can varnish the base, or paint it black.

STEP 2: MAKING THE METAL SUPPORTS

1: Cut three pieces of wire from a metal coat hanger, as shown in the drawing, using the pliers. Try not to bend the wires as they are cut. The long piece, for the backbone support, is 12½ inches (32 cm) long. The two shorter pieces are 7½ inches (18.5 cm) and 6 inches (15 cm) long. These are for the front and back vertical supports, respectively.

2: Take one of the short pieces and choose the end that is the least straight (if there is one). Using the pliers, bend the last ⅜ inch (1 cm) over until the end is about ⅜ inch (1 cm) from touching the rest. Hook the open loop over a piece of leftover

WARNING ▼▼▼

Youngsters should have the assistance of an adult helper to do the cutting and bending in this sec-

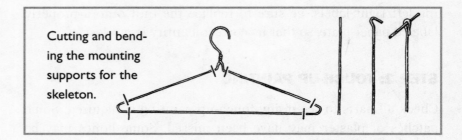

Cutting and bending the mounting supports for the skeleton.

coat hanger and bend the loop closed. Remove the leftover piece of coat hanger.

3: If necessary, straighten the vertical support wires if they were distorted during the bending. As an option, you can file a point on the unlooped end. This makes it easier to push the verticals into the holes you will drill into in the wooden board when mounting the skeleton.

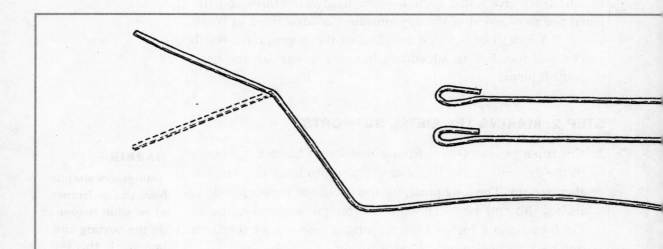

The backbone support and vertical supports, drawn actual size.

Repeat steps 2–3 for the second short piece of coat hanger.

To bend the backbone support into the shape shown in the drawing, do the following:

1: Measure 40 mm from one end. Grip firmly with the pliers, and bend the wire into the angle shown (about 150 degrees). This is a larger angle than the final one, and is to allow the vertebrae to be threaded on without getting stuck at the bend. It will be adjusted in a later section.

2: Measure 37 mm from the first bend and make a second one, as shown (118 degrees). Try to keep all bends in the same plane, so that when you are finished, the wire lies flat on the table.

3: Measure 125 mm from the second bend and mark with a magic marker or piece of tape. Bend the wire into a gentle arc between this mark and the second bend. (**Hint:** Hold the wire

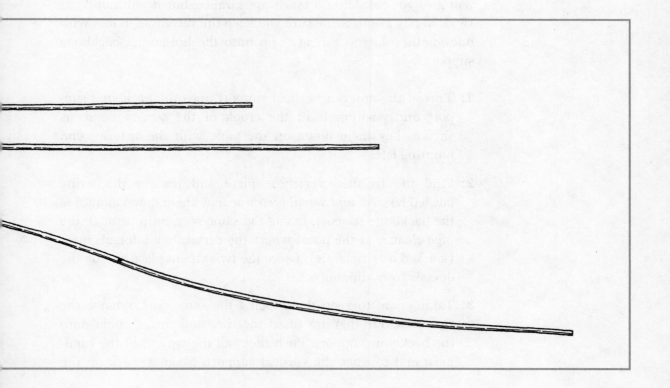

in both hands and use your thumbs for the bending—bend a little, move on a little, bend some more, move on a little, and so on.)

4: Make a second gentle bend in the opposite direction, between the mark and the end of the wire.

▼▼▼ Assembling the Skeleton

STEP 1: MOUNTING THE VERTEBRAE

In this section you'll be threading the individual vertebrae onto the horizontal backbone support and attaching this to the two vertical supports. My friends in Colorado tell me to be more adventurous and dispense with the anterior vertical support. You can do this if you like, and use only the posterior support. This will give your skeleton a racier appearance, but it will not be as rigid. In any event, make sure you keep the vertebrae in line with one another as you thread them onto the horizontal backbone support.

1: Thread the anterior vertical support onto the backbone support and position it in the crook of the second bend, as shown. Lay them down on the table with the anterior end pointing left.

2: Find the finished vertebrae plate and remove the string labeled *cervical and dorsal vertebrae*. Lay them down alongside the backbone support, facing the same way. Snip through the pipe cleaner at the point where the cervical and dorsals meet (marked by a twist tie). Leave the twist tie in place to stop the dorsals from slipping off.

3: Taking care to keep them facing the same way, remove the five vertebrae that are fused together and thread them onto the backbone support. Push them all the way until the hindmost end touches the vertical support. Make a mark on the

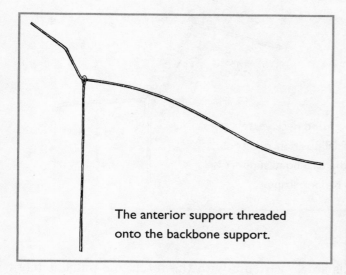

The anterior support threaded onto the backbone support.

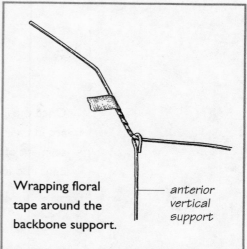

Wrapping floral tape around the backbone support.

anterior vertical support

backbone support to show how far forward they extend, then remove them.

4: Cut off a 6-inch (15 cm) length of floral tape and wrap it tightly around the backbone support to cover the section occupied by the vertebrae you just removed.

5: Replace the vertebrae. You'll have to rock them from side to side to slide them over the tape—they need to be a tight fit. Add more tape if they are too loose. Remove some of the tape if they are too tight. Push them all the way until they touch the vertical support.

6: Look at them from the front. You'll see a large gap between the backbone support and the inside edge of the neural canal. Cut off several 1-inch (2.5 cm) lengths of floral tape. Using your finger and thumb, roll these into tight scrolls. Pack these into the space between the *top* of the backbone support and the inside edge of the neural canal.

7: Remove the most posterior cervical vertebra from the pipe cleaner. Thread it onto the backbone support, with its posterior end facing toward the vertical support. Check the align-

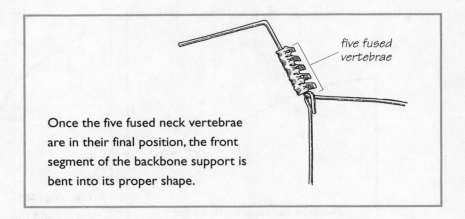

five fused
vertebrae

Once the five fused neck vertebrae
are in their final position, the front
segment of the backbone support is
bent into its proper shape.

ment of this single vertebra with the fused one immediately
behind it. The tops of their neural spines should be on about
the same level. If they do not line up well, modify the packing
of floral tape inside the fused vertebrae, raising or lowering
the most anterior one as required. When satisfied with the
alignment, remove the single vertebra.

8: Using pliers, decrease the angle of the first bend in the backbone support, as shown in the illustration.

9: Cut off 1 inch (2.5 cm) of floral tape and wrap it obliquely
and tightly around the backbone support so that it is only one
layer thick. Replace the vertebra, making sure its posterior
end faces toward the vertical support. It will be a tight fit.
Rock it from side to side as you push it along. Only remove
some of the floral tape if absolutely necessary to thread it on.

10: Add the remaining cervical vertebrae, ending with the most
anterior in the series.

During the next series of steps you will be adding the posterior
vertical support. If you opted to use both vertical supports, make
sure to keep them parallel to each other, and in their correct
relationship with the backbone support. Check this by looking
at the drawing on page 144 from time to time. Also, measure the

distance between the two vertical supports to make sure it is the same at their tops as it is at their bottoms.

1: Untie the twist tie from the pipe cleaner. Remove the first dorsal vertebra and thread it onto the tail end of the backbone support, keeping its anterior end facing the vertical support.

2: Making sure to keep the vertical support in its proper relationship with the backbone support, push the first dorsal vertebra all the way up until it contacts the vertical support.

3: Check the fit between the last cervical and first dorsal vertebrae. It may be necessary to file a little from the anterior edge of the neural spine of the dorsal vertebra. When satisfied with the fit, remove the dorsal vertebra and wrap the backbone support with floral tape as outlined in the next step.

4: Cut off 1 inch of floral tape. Wrap it tightly around the backbone support so it overlaps only itself. This gives a band the same width as the tape. Add a vertebra. Wrap another band of tape, overlapping the previous one by about 2 mm. Add another vertebra—and so on.

5: Add all thirteen dorsal and all five sacral vertebrae. Make sure that each additional vertebra is fitted flush to the one in front. Also, make sure that the vertical support retains its proper relationship with the backbone support.

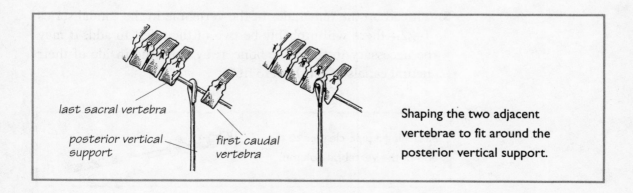

last sacral vertebra

posterior vertical support

first caudal vertebra

Shaping the two adjacent vertebrae to fit around the posterior vertical support.

6: Thread the posterior vertical support onto the backbone support and push it all the way, until it contacts the last sacral vertebra. Because of the angle between the posterior vertical and the backbone support, it is not possible to obtain anything like a flush fit. You will need to file a wedge of bone from the posterior surface of the last sacral vertebra, as shown. To get an idea of what needs to be filed, draw a line on the side of the centrum, parallel to the vertical support. Proceed by trial and error until you have a good fit.

7: Repeat step 6 for the first caudal vertebra, filing down its anterior surface.

8: Thread all but the last two caudal vertebrae from the string labeled *caudals 1–22*. This will leave 5–10 mm of the backbone support projecting beyond the last caudal added. If you run out of backbone support before you reach this stage, don't worry—just add the pipe cleaner earlier. If you have less of a projection, take one or more of the caudals off.

The backbone support now has to be extended. Do the following:

WARNING ▼▼▼

Not to be done by youngsters.

1: Take a pipe cleaner and, using a match, burn off 20 mm of cloth from one end, baring the underlying wire.

2: Push the bared wire through the gap between the last vertebra on the backbone support and the support itself. Keep pushing until the cloth part of the pipe cleaner is level with the end.

3: Thread on the remainder of the vertebrae in the caudal series 1–22—there will probably be two of them left to add. It may be necessary to file some bone away from the inside of their neural canals to get them to fit.

Attaching a pipe cleaner to the end of the vertebral column.

STEP 2: ATTACHING THE VERTEBRAL COLUMN TO THE WOODEN BASE

You are now ready to mount the skeleton onto the wooden base, but before doing so, you have to glue the vertical supports in place. The best way of doing this is to first temporarily mount the partially built skeleton onto a piece of Styrofoam. Alternatively, you can use the lid of a shoebox. Do the following:

1: Holding one vertical support in each hand, lower them until their ends make contact with the lid of the shoebox, or with the surface of the Styrofoam. Make sure that the vertical supports are vertical, them stab them into the surface.

How does your vertebral column look? Are the verticals really vertical?

2: Cover the table with a piece of clear plastic, like Saran Wrap, or a plastic bag (this is to stop the glue from sticking the specimen to the surface).

3: Lay the specimen on its side on top of the plastic. Line up the lower ends of the vertical supports with the edge of the table, using the latter as a horizontal reference line. Make sure the verticals are parallel with one another by making sure that the distances between them are the same at the top and bottom. It may be necessary to bend the top loop of one or both of the vertical supports relative to the rest of the support to get a better relationship with the backbone support.

4: Add a few drops of Krazy Glue to the contact areas between the vertical supports and the backbone support and the vertebrae. Allow to set for ten minutes. Check to see if the verticals are set in place. If necessary, glue again.

5: When satisfied, flip the specimen over and repeat step 4 on the other side.

Your specimen can now be attached to the wooden base. Do the following:

1: Push both verticals through the temporary base, so that their tips extend beyond the underside.

2: Maneuver the specimen into position above the wooden base, so that it occupies a central position. Because the tail is so much longer than the head and neck, the vertical supports will be much closer to one end of the base than to the other. As a rough guide, the anterior vertical support of my specimen was about 4 inches (10 cm) from one end, while the posterior support was about 9 inches (22 cm) from the same end.

3: Make small pencil crosses on the wooden base at the point where the two vertical supports make contact. Drill two holes at the crosses. This can be done using the points of the nail scissors, or, preferably, an electric drill (use a $5/64$-inch bit). The holes must not be any wider than the coat hanger; otherwise the vertical supports will not fit tightly into the base. The holes should be drilled to a depth that is about $1/8$ inch (3 mm) less than that of the thickness of the board. If you are using an electric drill, this is best done by measuring off the required depth from the tip of the drill bit and marking this with a piece of masking tape. Drill down into the wooden base until the masking tape marker just touches the surface.

4: Firmly grip the straight end of one of the vertical supports with the pliers, about $3/4$ inch (2 cm) from its end, and push it into the hole as far as it will go. It should be a tight fit, and the vertical support should be firm. If it is loose, pull it out and make the hole deeper.

5: Check the distance between the top surface of the wooden base and the top of the anterior and posterior vertical supports. These must be $6^{1}/4$ inches (16 cm) and $4^{3}/4$ inches (12 cm) respectively. If either one is less, ease it out of the hole a little. If the distance is greater, deepen the hole, or if need be, snip a little off the end of the vertical support.

STEP 3: FINISHING THE TAIL

1: Find the string of manufactured caudal vertebrae, labeled *caudals 23–45*. Starting at the anterior end (at caudal vertebra number 23), string as many of them onto the pipe cleaner as you can. Push them tightly against those that have already been mounted. I managed to thread twelve onto the pipe cleaner before the opening in the tail vertebrae became too narrow.

2: Snip the pipe cleaner flush with the last vertebra you managed to thread on.

3: Measure off a piece of twist tie that is about ½ inch (1 cm) longer than the combined lengths of the remaining tail vertebrae. Strip off the plastic and straighten the wire.

4: Thread the remaining caudal vertebra onto the wire, leaving the first ½ inch (1 cm), or so, bare. They will probably be a fairly tight fit.

5: Glue any loose vertebrae to the wire with Krazy Glue. Also glue the last one. Snip the wire off flush with the posterior end of the last vertebra. Allow to dry for about ten minutes.

6: Attach this string of vertebrae by pushing the bare wire into the gap between the end of the pipe cleaner and the inside edge of the last vertebra. Push it all the way until the vertebrae are touching. Glue in place with Krazy Glue.

STEP 4: CONSOLIDATING THE SACRUM

In life, the dinosaur's sacral vertebrae were firmly united, forming a strong attachment area for the pelvis. You similarly want to consolidate the sacrum of your model.

1: Measure the maximum height of your partial skeleton, from the top of the table to the top of the vertebral support. Make two piles of books, each one a few inches greater than this height. Place them about 4 inches (10 cm) closer together than the length of the wooden base.

2: Turn your specimen upside down, resting each end of the base on the pile of books.

3: Run several threads of glue along the underneath surfaces of the sacral vertebrae, thereby joining them together. Allow to set for about an hour. Stand the partial skeleton upright again.

STEP 5: MOUNTING THE PELVIS

Before gluing the left and right halves of the pelvis together you need to check that they fit together properly. Just to remind yourself which way the two halves of the pelvis go, see the drawing on page 113.

Hold the right half of the pelvis in your left hand with the front end pointing toward you. Do the same for the left side in your right hand. Line the two ilia up together so that they just touch and so that their anterior ends are on the same level. The tips of the other two bones (the pubis in front and the ischium behind) should touch their opposite partners. If necessary, adjust the positions of the bones until they do all line up. This is done by applying gentle pressure to the bones that need repositioning—there should be enough resilience in the cement holding them together to allow them to move slightly. It is most unlikely that you will get a perfect fit between each boot of the pubis. Don't worry, that will be fixed later. You may want to get the help of a second pair of hands for the next part.

1: Cut off a 7-inch (18 cm) length of twist tie. Hold the two halves of the pelvis together in one hand, lined up as they were when you were checking them. Thread the twist tie through both hip sockets.

2: Keeping the twist tie straight for the moment, put the pelvis beneath the vertebral column, making sure that the front end faces toward the neck. Adjust the position of the two halves of the pelvis so that:

1. The hip sockets are lined up with the vertical support, as shown in the drawing.

2. The inside surfaces of the left and right ilia are touching the vertebrae, as illustrated.

3. The top edges of the two ilia are only about $\frac{1}{16}$ inch (2 mm) above the level of the tops of the neural spines of the sacral vertebrae.

4. The tips of the left and right pubes touch each other.

5. The tips of the left and right ischia touch each other (the ischia embrace the vertical supports).

When you're sure that the pelvis is in the correct position, hold it in place with one hand and use the other hand to bend the ends of the twist tie upward. Bring the two ends together and twist them. Keep on twisting to take up the slack—this will hold the pelvis in the proper position. Gently let go of the pelvis,

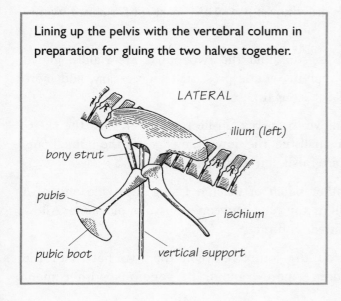

Lining up the pelvis with the vertebral column in preparation for gluing the two halves together.

LATERAL

ilium (left)

bony strut

pubis

ischium

pubic boot   vertical support

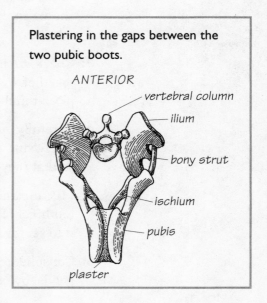

Plastering in the gaps between the two pubic boots.

ANTERIOR

vertebral column

ilium

bony strut

ischium

pubis

plaster

making sure that it does not move when you do so. If there is any movement, you can adjust the position of the pelvis by crimping the twist tie. You may find it useful to add a second loop of twist tie. Once the pelvis is fixed in its proper position it is ready for gluing. You'll be gluing the two halves of the pelvis together, but the whole thing will not be glued to the vertebral column just yet. Do the following.

Using a toothpick, add beads of glue to all the points of contact between the two halves of the pelvis. Be especially generous when gluing the two pubic boots together, adding the glue to their inside surfaces, where it will not show. Leave to set for at least half an hour.

The two halves of the pelvis will now be joined together, but the pelvic girdle will not be rigid. It has to be rigid for the modifications that are needed on the pubic boot.

1: Mix up a small amount of plaster (less than a level spoonful) with a few drops of cold water in a paper cup to make a thick paste.

2: Using the wide end of a toothpick, apply some of the plaster to the inside edges of the lowermost part of the two pubes, as shown in the drawing on page 135. Let it set for about twenty minutes.

3: Check to make sure that the two pubes are rigidly joined together by applying gentle pressure. If necessary, add more plaster and let it set again.

4: Carefully remove the pelvic girdle from the rest of the skeleton. Using a small file, file down the edges of the pubic boots so that they are flush, left with right.

5: Mix up another batch of plaster. Using the wide end of a toothpick, fill in any gaps between the two pubic boots. Allow it to set for fifteen minutes.

6: Consolidate all the joints between the two halves of the pelvis by adding more cement. Be generous with cement around the strut bridging the gap between the pubis and ilium, and in the joint between the ilium and ischium—excess glue will not show in the end. Wait a few minutes for the glue to begin to set.

7: Attach the pelvis to the rest of the skeleton again, as you did before, taking care to line everything up again. When satisfied with the fit, use a toothpick to add beads of glue to all the points where the pelvis touches against the vertebral column. Use enough glue to make a good solid job of it.

STEP 6: MOUNTING THE RIBS

Check to make sure that the glue affixing the pelvis to the vertebrae has dried. If it hasn't, let it set for another half hour, then try again.

Try gently moving the pelvis to see whether it is firmly attached. If in doubt, add more glue and leave it for an hour to set.

When you are sure the pelvis is well glued to the vertebrae, remove the twist tie and get ready to mount the ribs.

Cut two pieces of twist tie, each 10 inches (25 cm) long, and bend them into the shape shown in the drawing. Attach the ends of each twist tie to the vertical supports. These curved shapes are for supporting the ribs while they are being glued.

Find the finished ribs plate. The ribs are arranged, in pairs, in correct order, starting with the most anterior pair. Start with the set of left ribs. Prop up the base of your dinosaur skeleton so that the right side leans toward the table and the left side faces you. Do the following:

1: Look at the first rib. As you saw earlier, the ribs are forked, with one branch shorter than the other. The short branch attaches to the transverse process of the vertebra, while the long branch attaches to the side of the vertebra—take a look at the illustration on page 77 to remind yourself. Hold the rib up to the first dorsal vertebra (the one immediately behind the front vertical support) and try articulating its two branches.

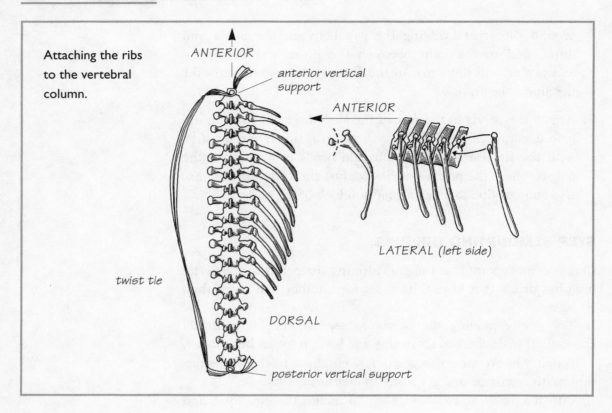

Attaching the ribs to the vertebral column.

ANTERIOR

anterior vertical support

ANTERIOR

LATERAL (left side)

twist tie

DORSAL

posterior vertical support

You may get a good fit, with the rib curving downward and backward. However, it may be necessary to use the nail clippers to snip about 2 mm off the end of the longest branch of the fork to get a good fit, as shown in the drawing. You can improve the fit by filing a shallow depression in the end of the upper branch of the rib to conform to the curvature of the end of the transverse process. When you're satisfied with the fit, move on to the next step.

2: Cut a ½-inch (1 cm) square of masking tape and stick it, sticky side out, to the twist-tie rib support, in the position that the rib will occupy. (Sticky side faces away from the vertebral column.)

3: Using a toothpick, put a bead of glue onto the ends of each of the two branches of the rib, and on their points of contact with the vertebra. Allow the glue to dry for a minute or so, then attach the rib to the vertebra, as you did in the previous step, so that it curves downward and backward. While holding the rib steady in one hand, attach the other end to the masking tape square to hold it in place. Once you've attached the rib with the tape you can let go. If need be, you can add more glue with a toothpick.

4: Repeat steps 1–3 for each of the other ribs in their turn.

Don't expect your dinosaur's ribs to be all lined up perfectly parallel to one another—they won't be! Nor are they evenly spaced in real dinosaur skeletons, not unless the ribs have been modeled in some other material. This is because the ribs, being relatively thin, and being curved in two planes, are readily broken and distorted during fossilization. Fossil ribs therefore seldom retain their original shape, so having uneven ribs in your skeleton will make it look all the more authentic.

Repeat steps 1–4 for the ribs of the right side.

Stand the partial skeleton upright again, with the base flat on the table. Allow at least an hour for the glue to harden. While you're waiting you can do the following.

STEP 7: MOUNTING THE BACK LEGS

Find the finished legs and feet plate.

1: Take the left femur and left tibia and fibula, and line them up as shown in the illustration. Add glue to their contact surfaces, wait one minute, then glue them together. Prop up with a small ball of plasticine while the glue sets.

2: Repeat step 1 for the right side.

3: Wait about ten minutes for the glue to dry. The joints will not be rigid because the glue is still flexible.

4: Make a ball of plasticine, about 1 inch (2.5 cm) in diameter.

5: Find the left foot. Position the left femur as shown in the

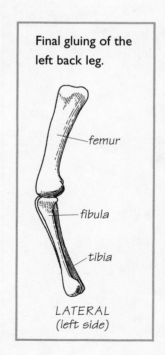

Final gluing of the left back leg.

femur

fibula

tibia

LATERAL
(left side)

drawing, tucking the head of the femur as tightly as you can into the hip socket. Position the foot as shown, too. You do not have to try to match the position of the leg segments exactly as shown in the drawing; it is only to give you an idea of what it should look like. Remember that when an animal is in motion its limb segments get into all sorts of positions, any one of which is "correct." When satisfied, remove the foot, keeping the rest of the leg in position. Position the plasticine ball beneath the lower end of the metatarsus, and press it against the wooden base. Adjust the ball so that it holds this lower end in place.

6: Without moving the leg any more than you have to, move the head of the femur out of the hip socket so that you can add glue to their points of contact. Be liberal with the glue. Allow it to dry for about one minute, then glue them together. Leave them to set for thirty minutes.

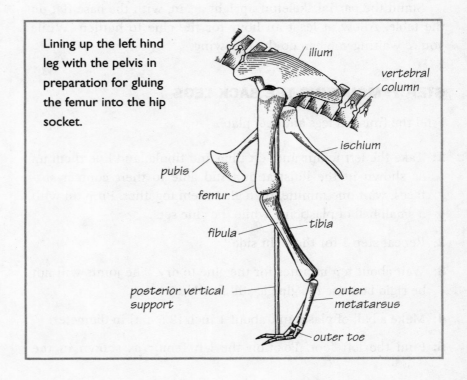

Lining up the left hind leg with the pelvis in preparation for gluing the femur into the hip socket.

ilium

vertebral column

ischium

pubis

femur

tibia

fibula

posterior vertical support

outer metatarsus

outer toe

7: Repeat steps 1–6 for the right side.

8: Remove the plasticine ball from the lower end of the left leg. Take care not to move the position of the leg because it will not be rigidly attached to the pelvis.

9: Position the left foot beneath the metatarsus, as shown in the illustration. You will be able to swing the foot back and forth to get the posture you want. When satisfied, use the plasticine ball to hold the foot in position. Separate the contact between the metatarsus and top of the foot so that you can add glue to both surfaces. Wait one minute for the glue to dry, then press them into contact. Using a toothpick, add beads of glue to the joint.

10: Repeat step 9 for the right side.

11: Consolidate the hip joint, and all of the joints in the leg, with additional beads of glue.

Allow the legs and feet to set for at least an hour. Meanwhile, you can do the following.

STEP 8: MOUNTING THE SKULL

1: Slip the skull onto the end of the backbone support. The front end of the support lies above the bony shelf between the tips of the upper jaws. The anterior end of the backbone support fits into the notch in the plate at the back end of the skull. Push the skull back until it contacts the first neck vertebra. When satisfied with the fit, remove the skull.

2: Liberally coat the entire end section of the backbone support (all the bare metal parts) with glue. Liberally coat the top surface of the bony shelf with glue. Apply a bead of glue to the notch at the back of the skull. Wait one minute for the glue to dry, then replace the skull. Make sure the front end of the vertebral support is firmly pressed against the top of the bony shelf. Allow to dry for thirty minutes, then consolidate with additional glue.

STEP 9: MOUNTING THE SHOULDERS

Make sure the glue holding the ribs is set and that all the ribs are firmly in place. If necessary, add more glue to consolidate any loose ribs, allowing thirty minutes for them to dry. Carefully undo the masking tape used to steady the ribs and remove the two twist ties to which the ribs were attached.

You're now ready to attach the shoulders. Find the pectoral girdle and limbs plate.

1: Prop up the base of your dinosaur, as you did when gluing the ribs, with the left side of the skeleton facing you.

2: Find the left scapulocoracoid and lay it at an angle across the first five ribs, as shown in the illustration (page 144). Arrange the scapula so that its top end is about ⁵⁄₁₆ inch (7 mm) below the neural spines of the dorsal vertebrae; the anterior end of the coracoid should be level with the front vertical support.

3: Make a note of the approximate points of contact between the ribs and the scapula. Remove the scapula, apply dabs of glue to the contact areas, and allow to dry for a minute or so.

4: Return the scapula to the ribs, make any final adjustments, then allow the glue to dry. Using a toothpick, apply beads of glue to the contact areas, and allow these to dry for at least half an hour.

Repeat steps 1–4 for the other side.

When both shoulders have set, stand your dinosaur skeleton upright again.

STEP 10: MOUNTING THE FORELIMBS

Find the two front limbs on the *pectoral girdle and limbs* plate.

1: Hold the left front limb in position, with the top end of the humerus in contact with the notch on the lower edge of the scapulocoracoid, as shown in the illustration. Position the forelimb so that it looks realistic (see the illustration of the completed skeleton on page 144 for inspiration).

2: When satisfied, hold the humerus firmly against the scapulocoracoid and add a droplet of Krazy Glue to their point of contact. Keep holding until the glue sets. This will probably take a matter of seconds, but hold in place for one minute just to make sure. When you let go, the limb should be secure. If not, add another droplet of Krazy Glue, making absolutely sure that the top of the humerus is pressed against the scapulocoracoid.

Gluing the left forelimb to the scapulocoracoid.

Repeat steps 1–2 for the right side.

STEP 11: ADDING THE CHEVRON BONES

Find the plastic bag containing the chevron bones on the finished vertebrae plate. These are to be added to caudal vertebrae 3 through 24, as shown in the illustration. The exact number is not critical, so if you want to add a few more, do so.

1: Arrange the chevrons in order of decreasing size.

2: Select an appropriate chevron for the first caudal in the series 3–24. Using the tweezers, hold it in its appropriate position beneath the caudal vertebra, sloping back at an angle, as shown, and firmly pressed against the vertebra. Add a droplet of Krazy Glue and hold it in place until the glue sets.

Repeat step 2 for the remaining caudals in the series. Select appropriately sized chevrons so that they diminish in length throughout the series.

Gluing the chevrons to the caudal vertebrae.

caudal vertebra 3

caudal vertebra 24

If you like, you can spray-paint your entire skeleton. Choose a dark brown, to give it a natural fossil bone color. The first painted skeleton I ever saw was a skeleton of *Apatosaurus* that Josh had built, using the previous book in the series. It looked really sharp. He painted all three of his succession of King Richards.

This completes your skeleton of *Tyrannosaurus rex*. I hope you are suitably impressed with your efforts! Each skeleton is unique, a little different from all the others, which is why I give them their own individual names. My first *T. rex*, Norman, appears on the cover of this book. I am always interested in hearing how others have got on with the building. If you'd like to send a photograph of your creation to me at the museum, I'd love to see it.

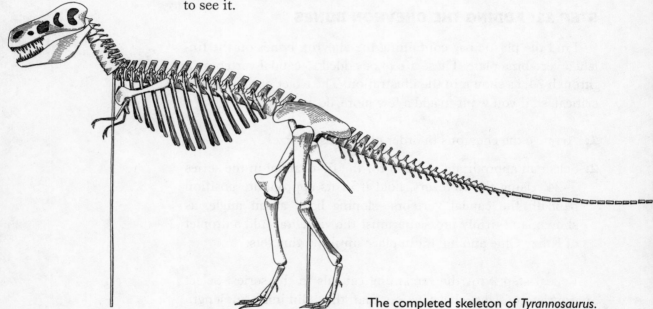

The completed skeleton of *Tyrannosaurus*.

Part 3

The Tyrant Lizard

When Sue, the *Tyrannosaurus* skeleton, came under the auctioneer's hammer in the fall of 1997, the whole world seemed to be watching. We certainly were at the Royal Ontario Museum. This was the most complete skeleton of *Tyrannosaurus* ever found, and we would have loved to purchase it. But, in the absence of a wealthy sponsor, it was well beyond our reach. We did get a copy of Sotheby's splendid sale catalogue, though, which was the closest we would ever get to the specimen. The inmates of the Palaeobiology Department tried guessing the price it might sell for. My guess was $1.6 million, which I suspected was on the high side. We were all astounded at the final hammer price of $7.6 million—sold to the Field Museum in Chicago. *Tyrannosaurus* has great people appeal.

What is it about *Tyrannosaurus* that we find so captivating? It may be similar to the fascination we have for sharks—those cold, merciless, unstoppable killers. And *Tyrannosaurus* was one of the largest predators ever to stalk the earth. To stand beside any large dinosaur skeleton is an awe-inspiring sensation. But when you stand beside *Tyrannosaurus* and look up at that massive skull— those daggerlike teeth that could pulverize you like a mechanical rock crusher—you can almost feel the brute strength of the beast. And who can forget that scene in *Jurassic Park* when the jeep is being chased, at great speed, by a charging *T. rex*?

How realistic is this image of *Tyrannosaurus*? Was it a hot-blooded predator chasing down its prey like a hunting lion, or was it less active, like a skulking crocodile? Perhaps it did not hunt at all, but was instead a scavenger, feeding on carrion, as some paleontologists have suggested. To try and find answers to these questions of the remote past, we first need to look at the living world.

Like other mammals, and birds, we are warm-blooded, maintaining high and relatively constant body temperatures regardless of **ambient** (surrounding) **temperatures**. The heat comes from within our body cells, and this thermal strategy is described as being **endothermic**, meaning *inside heat*. Reptiles, in contrast, do not maintain high constant body temperatures, and are often referred to as being cold-blooded. This is because their body cells produce only about one-tenth the amount of heat as that produced by the cells of endothermic animals—they have lower metabolic rates, as mentioned earlier. Reptiles are cold and therefore sluggish at night, when the temperature falls, and they warm up during the day by basking in the sun. As their major source of heat is from outside the body, they are said to be **ectothermic** (*outside heat*).

Reptiles generally (there are some exceptions) lack **stamina**—the ability to maintain high levels of activity for extended periods of time. Consequently, predatory reptiles typically adopt a sit-and-wait hunting strategy. Crocodiles, for example, float like dead logs, waiting for unsuspecting prey to venture into the water, while snakes bide their time coiled beneath fallen trees and the like. But when the moment comes, these static life forms burst into action with all the speed and fury of the swiftest endotherms.

We mammals tend to be elitist, judging the reptiles' cold-blooded limitations as inferior to our warm-blooded readiness. But we pay a price for our high activity levels, consuming about ten times more food, weight for weight, than a similarly sized reptile. We should also bear in mind that it is often a bird or a mammal that finishes up inside a reptile's stomach. And although reptiles spend much of their time inactive, they can move very fast when they want to: a lunging crocodile is every bit as fast as a charging lion. But most reptiles can keep up their bursts of activity only for brief intervals of time before becoming exhausted. Their exhaustion is followed by a long period of inactivity, during which time they are unresponsive. This is due to the accumulation of lactic acid in their muscles—the cause of our own stiffness after strenuous exercise.

Significantly, a reptile's endurance is proportional to its size. This was dramatically demonstrated in an experiment conducted by some biologists in Australia. Crocodiles of different body sizes were lassoed, then allowed to thrash around in the water until they were exhausted. The smallest individuals (under 1 kg, or 2 lb) became exhausted in about five minutes, whereas the largest ones (over 100 kg, or 200 lb) took over thirty minutes. Once exhausted, the crocodiles were incapable of any activity for upward of several hours (seemingly regardless of size), while their bodies broke down the accumulated lactic acid. While the crocodiles were in this state they were unresponsive—the experimenters could have tweaked their toothy snouts without fear of retribution. Contrast this slow recovery after strenuous activity with the quick recovery of mammals. A cheetah's three-hundred-yard dash after a gazelle may leave it exhausted and panting, but it can still defend itself, and is fully recovered within minutes. This is because mammals, and birds, are able to break down lactic acid much more rapidly than reptiles.

Paleontologist Robert Bakker, who championed the idea that dinosaurs were hot-blooded, maintains that all dinosaurs had high metabolic rates and high activity levels, like modern birds and mammals. His influence has been enormous, as evidenced by numerous TV specials and Spielberg's movies, where dinosaurs are depicted as running and leaping with the speed and agility of antelopes. Although some dinosaurs, like small theropods, may have been endothermic, including the ones most closely related to birds, the idea that *all* dinosaurs, or even many dinosaurs, were endothermic is unfounded.

One of the major advantages of being endothermic is that an animal is always at its optimum body temperature for maximal activity, regardless of ambient temperatures. If a sleeping mammal is disturbed on a cool night it flees, or attacks, almost instantly. But a cold, sluggish reptile remains that way until warmed by the morning sun. Exceptions to this are those reptiles whose body mass is sufficiently large for them to retain some of their body heat overnight. The mechanism involved has to do with the relationship between areas and volumes, and the fact that heat is lost through surfaces. As things get bigger, their surface area becomes increasingly smaller relative to their volume. A baked potato has a much larger volume than a pea, and therefore a relatively smaller surface area. This explains why a baked potato remains hot on your plate long after all the peas have grown cold.

I experienced the effect of size on a reptile's body temperatures during a trip to Galápagos. Our party had climbed to the top of a quiescent volcano, where we camped overnight. Although it had been uncomfortably hot during most of the day, it was pleasantly cool in the highlands. But when night fell the mercury dropped like a stone, and we were sorry there were no sleeping bags for the tents. When I awoke the following morning, cold and in need of coffee, I saw that a giant tortoise had wandered into camp. It was about the size of a washing machine, and if I had wrapped my arms around the top of its shell my fingers would barely have touched the ground on either side. (It was for these gargantuans that the archipelago was named.) The tortoise was about as inactive as I was, and when I put my cold mammalian fingers under his soft reptilian armpit, I found it was as warm as toast, as I had anticipated. The Galápagos tortoise weighs about 450 pounds (200 kg), which is small by dinosaurian standards. However, it is sufficiently large that its body temperature falls only about 5 Fahrenheit degrees (3 Celsius degrees) during the night, while ground temperatures fall about 36 Fahrenheit degrees (20 Celsius degrees). Their body temperatures therefore remain fairly constant throughout the twenty-four-hour period. So most dinosaurs could not have avoided having fairly constant and high body temperatures, by virtue of their large body mass. They could have enjoyed the advantage of being independent of the sun's heat because of this, without the high food costs. Furthermore, their large body mass would have enabled them to keep up bursts of activity, as when capturing prey, for extended periods before becoming exhausted from lactic acid accumulation—as in the largest crocodiles.

If dinosaurs *did* have high metabolic rates, like birds and mammals, they would not only have had large appetites, but would also have had the problem of shedding excess heat during extreme activity and during the heat of the day. Elephants, for example, because of their small surface area relative to their large volume, are prone to suffer from the heat. They avoid the noon-day sun, where possible, by seeking shade, and readily take to the water, if available. If the largest dinosaurs, the sauropods, had possessed high metabolic rates, it is inconceivable how they could have shed excess heat. Aside from these practical reasons why most, if not all, dinosaurs could not have been endothermic, there is also physical evidence to support the conclusion. This evidence concerns the breathing apparatus.

Mammals and birds, as we saw earlier, have large oxygen demands, which are met by their specialized lungs. The rapid uptake of oxygen and loss of carbon dioxide occurs at the moist internal surfaces of the lungs. When we inhale, the air first has to be humidified and warmed up to body temperature before entering the lungs. If the air were not humidified, it would tend to remove water from the surface of the lungs. And if the air were cold, it would cause the fine blood vessels, called **capillaries**, which lie next to the surface, to contract. This would reduce the blood flow, thereby reducing the rate of gaseous exchange. It is the contraction of the capillaries in our skin that causes our faces to become white on cold days.

I always marvel at how quickly the inhaled air can be heated and humidified, especially on a cold winter's day. The secret lies in the large volume of our nasal passages, and in the scroll-like turbinal bones, or **respiratory turbinates**, that occupy much of the space. The respiratory turbinates, and the inside surfaces of the nasal passages, are covered by a thin lining of cells, some of which produce moisture to keep the lining wet.

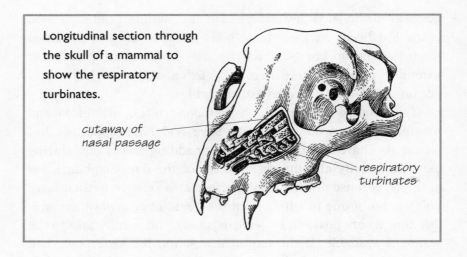

Longitudinal section through
the skull of a mammal to
show the respiratory
turbinates.

cutaway of
nasal passage

respiratory
turbinates

This moist layer is richly supplied with capillaries (hence nose-bleeds). The relatively large surface area of the turbinates insures that the inspired air is both humidified and warmed. With very few exceptions, all endotherms have respiratory turbinates (they are cartilaginous in birds), and relatively voluminous nasal passages. But respiratory turbinates are unknown in ectotherms. Furthermore, their nasal passages are only about one-quarter as voluminous as those of endotherms. John Ruben and his colleagues compared CAT scans through the skulls of a crocodile, an ostrich, a sheep, two theropods (*Nanotyrannus* and *Ornithomimus*), and a duck-billed dinosaur (*Hypacrosaurus*). Significantly, respiratory turbinates were absent from the crocodile and from all three dinosaurs. Their nasal passages were also relatively smaller than those of the two endotherms (ostrich and sheep). This is fairly conclusive evidence that the dinosaurs they studied were not endothermic. It should be noted that *Nanotyrannus*, whose name means *small tyrant,* looks like a scaled-down *Tyrannosaurus.* Indeed, there is evidence that it may represent a juvenile individual of *Tyrannosaurus.*

Given that most, if not all, dinosaurs lacked the high metabolic rates and high activity levels associated with endothermy, what do we visualize as the possible lifestyle of *Tyrannosaurus?* As almost everything we know of *Tyrannosaurus,* and every other extinct animal, is deduced from its skeletal remains, this is an appropriate place to begin to look for clues.

That *Tyrannosaurus* was a carnivore is in no doubt because it has all the attributes of a meat-eater: sharp teeth for slicing through flesh and sharp claws on the fingers and toes for slashing and grappling. The curved teeth are slightly flattened, giving them a somewhat oval cross-section, and they have serrated cutting edges running along their anterior and posterior margins, like a steak knife. Each tooth is embedded in a deep socket such that only about half of their total length is exposed. Having firmly rooted teeth would make it unlikely for them to be pulled out when the individual was biting and ripping through flesh. Bite marks are occasionally found on dinosaur bones, and these can sometimes give a clue as to what animals may have been feeding on the remains. One of the most informative examples of this is a series of puncture marks discovered on the pelvis and sacrum of a specimen of *Triceratops.* One of the puncture marks is sufficiently deep that the researchers could pour some molding material into the depression and make a cast of the tooth that had inflicted the damage. The shape of the resulting cast, which was only about an inch long (about 2.4 cm), closely matched that of the tip of a *Tyrannosaurus* tooth. The agreement in shape, taken with the large size, was fairly conclusive evidence that the bite marks had been made by a *Tyrannosaurus.* There were numerous bite marks, showing where the carnivore had repeatedly bitten down onto the *Triceratops* carcass, breaking off chunks of bone. Modern carnivores—like big cats, and especially hyenas—consume bone along with flesh; the bones provide minerals as well as proteins.

The *Triceratops* bone was of a similar density, and presumably similar strength, as that of a modern cow. The investigators therefore carried out some tests to estimate the biting forces that the *Tyrannosaurus* had inflicted on the *Triceratops.* They did this by making a metal cast of a *Tyrannosaurus* tooth and setting it up in an apparatus that drove it into the pelvic bone of a cow. By adjusting the force of the impact, they determined what bite

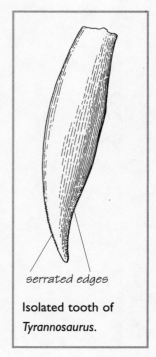

serrated edges

Isolated tooth of *Tyrannosaurus.*

force was necessary to produce puncture marks of similar depth to those found in the *Triceratops* bones. The estimated bite forces exceeded those generated by the lion, and were similar to those of the American alligator.

This investigation does not tell us whether *Tyrannosaurus* preyed on *Triceratops,* or merely scavenged its dead carcass. *Triceratops* would certainly have been a formidable adversary—it was armed with long, sharp horns and had an estimated weight of about 6 tons, which is comparable with that of an adult African elephant. (The African elephant is heavier than its Asian relative.)

Numerous estimates have been given for the body weight of *Tyrannosaurus,* ranging from just over 3 tons to over 7 tons. One of the most recent and carefully calculated estimates is 6 tons, which seems very plausible. This was based on a fairly complete skeleton of *Tyrannosaurus* that is in the Museum of the Rockies in Montana. This particular skeleton is of a slender build, and is one of two varieties that Paleontologist Ken Carpenter recognizes for *Tyrannosaurus.* The other form is the robust variety, which would have been heavier in life. It seems that the two varieties represent the two sexes, and Carpenter suggests that the heavier type represents the female. This is because the robust variety appears to have a wider gap between its ischium and tail, indicating a space for the passage of eggs.

▼▼▼

Differences between the sexes is called **sexual dimorphism** (*two forms*) and often includes size differences, as in our own species. Men tend to be both more heavily built and larger than women, and the same is also true for many other mammals, including big cats, bison, sea lions, polar bears, and toothed whales, like killer whales and sperm whales. Males are also larger than females in most birds. However, the reverse is true for birds of prey, where the female is sometimes as much as twice as heavy as the male, such as the sharp-shinned hawk. Similarly, the female is larger than the male in many mammals, including baleen whales, like the blue whale, and most hares and rabbits. Differences between robust and slender forms are not unique to *Tyrannosaurus;* the same has also been reported for the small dinosaur *Syntarsus,* from the Triassic rocks of southern Africa. Here again the robust form has been tentatively identified as the female.

The Museum of the Rockies skeleton of *Tyrannosaurus* is about 39 feet long (11.96 m), measured from the end of the snout to the tip of the tail. Sue, the largest skeleton of *Tyrannosaurus* ever found, is of the robust variety. Its length is not known for sure because it is still being worked upon, but it has been estimated at about 41 feet (12.6 m). Its live weight would probably have exceeded that of any African elephant.

Tyrannosaurus, like other theropods, walked on its hind legs. This **bipedal** (*two feet*) posture was also used by many other dinosaurs. The duck-billed dinosaurs, the **hadrosaurs**, walked on all fours, which is described as being **quadrupedal** (*four feet*), but they were probably bipedal when running. *Tyrannosaurus,* with its exceedingly small front legs, was obliged to be bipedal all the time. Bipedal locomotion requires all the weight to be carried

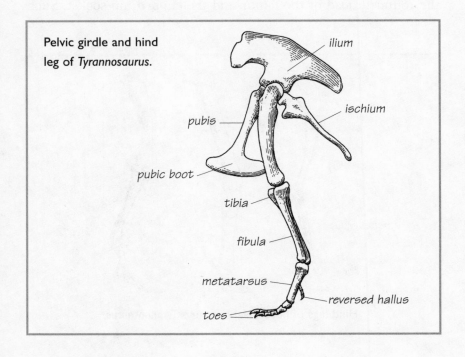

Pelvic girdle and hind leg of *Tyrannosaurus.*

ilium

ischium

pubis

pubic boot

tibia

fibula

metatarsus

reversed hallus

toes

by the hind legs, which are correspondingly larger than the front ones. The pelvic girdle is accordingly much larger than the pectoral girdle. This is also true for dinosaurs like hadrosaurs, which spent only part of their time being bipedal. The pelvic girdle of *Tyrannosaurus* is a massive structure, with a robust pubis ending in a huge pubic boot. People often confuse the pubis with the femur, because it is about the same size and occupies a similar position in the skeleton. One of the main functions of the pubis was to provide a large attachment area for muscles involved in maintaining posture and moving the femur back and forth. The pubic boot reaches down to the level of the knee, and marks the lowermost point on the animal's torso. The ischium, which is much smaller than the pubis, is quite slender, and was also for the attachment of muscles. Some of these muscles probably attached to the femur, and others to the base of the tail, providing for both posture and movement.

The other main function of the pelvis was to provide a firm foundation for attaching the legs to the body, via the hip joint. As in our own body, this is a ball-and-socket joint, formed between the rounded head of the femur and the cupped hip socket. Such

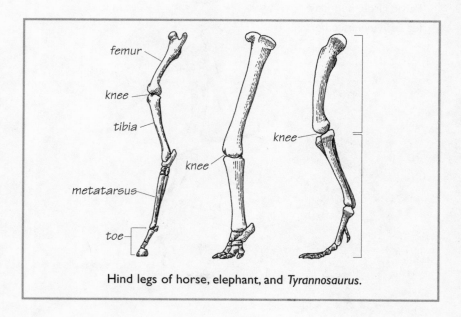

Hind legs of horse, elephant, and *Tyrannosaurus*.

joints give a great deal of freedom of movement, but this would have been limited by the muscles and ligaments attached to the femur. The massive ilium of *Tyrannosaurus* provided for a large contact area with the sacrum, to which it was rigidly attached. The entire body therefore pivoted about the hip socket, the long muscular tail acting as a counterbalance for the front part of the body.

The lower leg, from the knee down to the toes, is much longer than the upper segment, represented by the femur. This is suggestive of an ability to run, and is described as being a **cursorial** (*running*) feature. In the horse, for example, which is cursorial, the lower leg segment is much longer than the upper one. This is largely attributed to the elongation of the bones of the upper foot region (the metatarsus), and to the long (single) toe.

The elephant, in contrast, which is not cursorial, has a lower leg segment that is slightly shorter than the upper one. Elephants certainly do run, and can reach speeds of up to about 22 mph (35 km/h), which is about as fast as an Olympic sprinter. But they do this with an unusual straight-legged gait, which is really a fast walk. There is never more than one foot off the ground at any one time during this movement. Elephants never **trot** or **gallop**—gaits where there are never more than two feet on the ground at any one time. Trotting and galloping, which are restricted to quadrupeds, include brief intervals when all of the feet are off the ground. The reason why elephants restrict themselves to walking, even when "running," is to reduce the stresses on their bones. If you watch elephants at the zoo you'll notice that their movements are slow and deliberate, and the same is true in the wild. They also try to avoid moving over uneven terrain, taking great pains to avoid the possibility of falling over. This is because a fall for such a heavy animal is likely to result in serious injury, or even death.

So what sort of a runner was *Tyrannosaurus* likely to have been? According to some paleontologists, such as Robert Bakker and Greg Paul, *Tyrannosaurus* was a fast runner, capable of reaching speeds up to about 45 miles per hour (73 kilometers per hour)! Other paleontologists, like Tony Thulborn, suggest maximum speeds closer to 15 mph (24 km/h). The running speeds of dinosaurs have been deduced from measurements taken from fossil trackways. However, as I have explained in another book (*Dinosaurs, Spitfires, and Sea Dragons*), these calculations are based upon a number of untestable assumptions, and the equation upon which they are based has serious limitations. It is therefore not possible to deduce reliable speed estimates from dinosaur trackways. We should bear in mind that our data for the running speeds of living animals is far from complete, with precious few species for which we have accurate speed measurements. Estimating the speeds of animals that became extinct over 65 million years ago is therefore highly speculative, and all we can do is make some generalizations.

▼▼▼

An adult *Tyrannosaurus* weighed at least as much as a full-grown African elephant. It therefore seems unlikely that it would have been able to run any faster, based on considerations of bone stresses. Furthermore, as pointed out by Paleontologist Jim Farlow and his colleagues, serious consequences would have arisen from a fall by a running *Tyrannosaurus*. By estimating the damage that would likely occur at different speeds, they concluded that *Tyrannosaurus* was a slow runner. Their estimated top speed was comparable to that of an elephant, which is about as fast as a human sprinter. This seems entirely reasonable to me, but R. McNeil Alexander, a specialist in animal locomotion, reminds us that giraffes gallop at fairly high speeds (25 mph; 40 km/h). Although considerably lighter than a tyrannosaur, the giraffe is just as tall, and would presumably sustain severe injuries during a fall. Regardless of this, I cannot visualize *Tyrannosaurus* as pounding along in hot pursuit of its prey. Perhaps, like the elephant, it ran at an animated walk.

The front limbs seem ridiculously small compared with the rest of the skeleton, and they would have appeared abnormal in life, like birth defects. However, they are about as big as our own arms, and, judging from the well-developed muscle scars (the roughened areas on the bones where muscles attached), they were well muscled. Kangaroos also have relatively small arms, but they are deceptively strong. I learned this firsthand when I was mugged by a large kangaroo in an Australian game park! Intent on taking the bag of peanuts I was carrying, the kangaroo grabbed me from behind, pinning my arms to my sides. I could not break his grip, and the best I could manage was to shake some of the peanuts from the bag, causing him to let go and pick them up.

The front limbs of *Tyrannosaurus* are barely long enough to reach the mouth, even with the head bent down, and it is difficult to visualize their function. One suggestion is that the fingers may have been used as grapples to secure the front end of the body when a recumbent individual returned to its feet. Given that elephants seldom lie down, and then only for brief periods because of the risks of compressive tissue damage, *Tyrannosaurus* may not have lain down at all. Perhaps the forelimbs were used to grapple their prey. Alternatively, they may have been important when the individuals were young, when the forelimbs may have been much longer relative to the rest of the body. This situation, where parts of the body grow at different rates than the rest, is common, and is called **allometry** (meaning *different length*). The head, for example, is relatively large at birth and grows more slowly than the rest of the body, which is why babies have disproportionately large heads compared with adults.

The neck of the *Tyrannosaurus* is short, reducing the leverage of the huge head upon the body. It has well-developed cervical ribs and fairly long neural spines, which would have provided large attachment areas for the muscles. This is indicative of a powerful neck, which would have been required to support, and power, the massive head. The weight of the head was reduced by the large openings that perforate the skull, the bone being concentrated in regions exposed to the highest stresses. The deep skull and lower jaw, which accommodated the long roots of the teeth, also provided a large attachment area for the jaw muscles. The depth also added to the strength needed to withstand the powerful biting force, the same way that planks of wood are positioned sideways to bear the weight of the floors of a house. The orbits appear to have been directed forward somewhat, giving a small degree of overlap between the fields of view of the two eyes. This would have given *Tyrannosaurus* a degree of binocular vision, an attribute of considerable importance to predators. Cats and dogs, for example, have their eyes facing directly forward, as we do, giving good binocular vision and therefore good depth perception.

Was *Tyrannosaurus* an active predator, like a lion, that hunted and killed its prey, or was it a scavenger, feeding on carcasses? We will never know the answer for sure. We can only speculate by making comparisons with living animals.

Hyenas are primarily scavengers, and have powerful jaws with strong teeth. This allows them to chomp through bones as if they were nachos. *Tyrannosaurus* was similarly well endowed, as shown by the deep upper and lower jaws and the stout, deeply rooted teeth. The evidence from the *Triceratops* pelvis with tooth marks supports this conclusion. However, hunting and scavenging are by no means mutually exclusive, and hyenas, which were long thought to be scavengers that never hunted for themselves, are now known to be formidable predators. And many animals that kill for a living also take carrion when it is available. This is true of mammals and reptiles, as well as of birds of prey. I imagine that *Tyrannosaurus* would have hunted prey when the opportunity arose, feeding on carrion at other times.

Whether it pursued its prey, like most big cats and many birds of prey, or waited in ambush, like crocodiles and snakes and the Komodo dragon (a large lizard found only in Indonesia), is debatable. We have seen that reptiles generally lack stamina, obliging them to wait until their prey comes close, rather than chasing after them. It seems likely that the metabolic rate of *Tyrannosaurus* would have been low, more like that of modern reptiles. However, that does not necessarily rule out the possibility of their having pursued their prey. This is because large reptiles, as seen earlier, can keep up high levels of activity for fairly long periods of time before becoming exhausted. It has been suggested that carnivorous dinosaurs may have hunted in packs, a strategy used by lions and certain other mammalian carnivores to improve their hunting success. Although cooperative behavior of this kind is not normally associated with reptiles because of their lesser mental capacity, it is not unprecedented. Crocodiles, for example, sometimes cooperate in catching fishes by forming a semicircle around a river mouth. Each individual keeps to its own station, even though it might mean losing a fish to a neighbor, and there is no fighting over the spoils.

▼▼▼

Hadrosaurs were the most likely prey species of *Tyrannosaurus*. Not only were they among the most abundant herbivorous dinosaurs of the time, but they had no armor or weapons of defense. We have some direct evidence of this in a toe bone of the hadrosaur *Edmontosaurus* that bears tooth marks attributed to *Tyrannosaurus*. Hadrosaurs were about the same size as the Asian elephant, having an estimated body weight of 4 tons and averaging about 25 feet (8 m) in length. As in the case of the *Triceratops* with tooth marks, we do not know whether the specimen of *Edmontosaurus* was scavenged or actively killed.

While we can never know how *Tyrannosaurus* lived, we do know that it was one of the largest flesh-eaters ever to walk the Earth. When standing dwarfed beside a museum skeleton of

Restoration of *Tyrannosaurus*.

Tyrannosaurus, it is not difficult to let one's imagination fill in the blanks. This, surely, was an active predator rather than a scavenger. Dominated by the massive skull and scimitar teeth, the skeleton has all the attributes of a formidable killer. The robust talons of the massive feet could have ripped through hide and muscle with the same ease that the jaws rendered flesh and bone. But for all its large size, the skeleton is remarkably gracile. The femur and other hind limb bones are slender, and the pelvic girdle is strikingly narrow. This was a greyhound rather than a bulldog. But while possessing the attributes of a runner, *Tyrannosaurus* is more likely to have ambushed its prey like a crocodile than run down its quarry like a lion. And just imagine the tearing and biting and smashing that followed once contact had been made. There could be few sights on Earth to compare with the spectacle of a tyrannosaur going about its deadly business.

Recipes

The following recipes were specifically devised for this book. The Chicken Pot is very simple and didn't take much imagination, but I'm rather proud of the other two. The fajita recipe uses the meat obtained from boiling a chicken, as outlined on page 34. The other recipes start with whole uncooked chickens. These should be skinned first, which removes most of the fat. Also, try and remove most of the fat that underlies the skin. The skin should be saved and frozen for making stock.

▼▼▼FABULOUS FENNEL FAJITAS

Makes four fajitas, which should serve two. Preparation time and cooking time each about ten minutes.

1. Skin the avocado, slice it in half, and remove the stone. Cut each half into fine slices, not more than about ¹/₁₆ inch or 2 mm thick. Keep for later use.

2. Chop tomatoes into small cubes (¼ inch; 5 mm or less). Drain off and discard excess liquid. Keep tomatoes for later use.

3. Put some olive oil in a frying pan and heat at medium high. Add the chicken meat, breaking up with a spatula while browning. Sprinkle in ½ teaspoon of fennel. Keep stirring until lightly browned, adding more olive oil as necessary. Add lemon juice and another ½ teaspoon of fennel, stirring well. When most of the liquid has cooked off, add 2 tablespoons of sour cream and the last ½ teaspoon of fennel. Keep cooking until most of the remaining liquid cooks off. Remove from heat and stir in 2 tablespoons of sour cream.

▼▼▼▼▼▼▼▼▼▼▼▼▼▼▼

1 cup of boiled chicken

1 avocado

2 medium-size tomatoes

3 tablespoons of lemon juice

6 tablespoons of sour cream (preferably light) or yogurt

1½ teaspoons of powdered fennel

4 tortillas

About 3 tablespoons of olive oil

Salt, to taste

4. Add avocado slices, a few at a time, chopping well into mixture with spatula. Add tomato cubes and mix well. Return to heat for 2 minutes to warm.

5. Cut off a square of waxed paper, cover with a tortilla, and roll into a cigar, tucking in the two ends of paper to prevent unwrapping. Place in microwave on full power for 30 seconds to heat. Alternatively, wrap tortillas in foil and heat in oven set at 350 degrees for a few minutes.

6. Remove pan from heat. Spread ¼ of the mixture on each tortilla and roll up.

▼▼▼CHICKEN POT

Serves three to four. Preparation time about fifteen minutes; cooking time about one hour. An ideal winter meal.

▼▼▼▼▼▼▼▼▼▼▼▼▼▼▼

1 chicken
2 cans of consommé and
   1 can of water
1 large onion, finely
   chopped
1 teaspoon of rosemary
1 teaspoon of marjoram
3 tablespoons of
   cornstarch
¼ cup of red wine

1. Skin the chicken.

2. Put the chopped onion into a saucepan large enough to hold the chicken. Add the chicken, consommé, water, and spices. Bring to a boil, cover, and simmer for one hour.

3. Remove the chicken and place in a casserole dish. Any oil from chicken floating on the surface of the stock can be removed by dabbing gently with a kitchen towel. Strain the stock through a sieve and discard the onion. Blend the wine and cornstarch. Bring the stock to a boil in the saucepan. Add cornstarch and wine mixture while stirring vigorously. When the stock has thickened, remove from heat. Use stock as sauce when serving the chicken.

For extra body add 3 tablespoons of barley, lentils, split peas, or any other dried vegetables prior to cooking, and do not discard onions. Mashed potatoes are the recommended accompanying vegetable.

▼▼▼TANGY TYRANNOSAUR

This recipe is worth the price of the book.

Serves three to four. Preparation time about fifteen minutes; cooking time about one hour.

1. Skin the chicken.

2. Place the chicken, breast side down, into the freezer bag and add the lemon juice, soy sauce, white wine, and tarragon. Mix together. Squeeze out air and seal the bag securely.

You will notice that the marinade collects at the bottom of the bag without completely immersing the chicken. This can easily be remedied. Place the bag into a casserole or saucepan. Screw up a few sheets of newspaper and pack tightly around the bottom of the bag. This forces the marinade up and over the chicken.

3. Put the chicken into the refrigerator and leave to marinate overnight.

4. Drain off and save the marinade. Put the chicken, and ½ cup of the marinade, into a casserole dish previously sprayed with cooking oil. Tent with foil and cook in the oven at 350 degrees for an hour.

5. Pour the juice from the casserole dish into a glass or separator to settle. Separate and discard the top layer of oil. Add the rest to a saucepan with some of the saved marinade to make just over 1 pint. Add the bouillon cube and bring to a boil.

6. Blend the wine with cornstarch. Bring the stock in the pan to a boil and add the cornstarch mixture while stirring well. When sauce has thickened, remove from heat.

Serve with roast potatoes, roast parsnips, and green vegetables of choice.

1 chicken
½ cup of lemon juice
½ cup of light soy sauce
1½ cups of white wine
1 teaspoon of tarragon
1 medium freezer bag and twist tie
1 chicken bouillon cube
¼ cup of white (or red) wine
2 tablespoons of cornstarch
(Equal quantities of soy sauce and lemon juice can be substituted for the white wine if desired.)

Sixty Scintillating Topics for Discussion

1. What are the barbs of a feather, and how are they kept together?
2. What is a contour feather?
3. Why do some contour feathers have the rachis closer to the leading edge of the feather?
4. What is the furcula, and where is it found?
5. What is cladistics?
6. What is the reversed hallux?
7. Give one of the main differences between saurischian and ornithischian dinosaurs.
8. Name five theropods.
9. What is the diaphragm, and what is it used for?
10. What is metabolic rate?
11. Why is it important for our lungs to have a large internal surface area?
12. How is the internal surface area of our lungs made so large?
13. Give one major difference between the lungs of a mammal and those of a lizard.
14. How do lizards and snakes ventilate their lungs? How does this differ from the way we ventilate ours?
15. What are septate lungs, and which animals have them?
16. How is it that a chicken with a broken wing could still breathe if its trachea were blocked?
17. What are air sacs, and which animals have them?

18. Why does breathing in and out rapidly make us dizzy?
19. What is so unusual about the way crocodiles breathe?
20. Have feathered dinosaurs ever been found?
21. How would you define a bird?
22. Which two competing ideas explain the evolution of feathers?
23. Why do contour feathers, and hairs, have muscles?
24. How can some birds fly at altitudes so high that it would cause a mammal to become unconscious?
25. How does the hand of a bird embryo compare with that of a theropod such as *Allosaurus*?
26. What are sternal ribs?
27. What is convergence? Give an example.
28. Name two features that have been used to argue that birds are not theropod dinosaurs.
29. How could you tell if the chicken served to you in a restaurant was a mature bird?
30. What is the keel of a bird, and what is one of its main functions?
31. Under what circumstances would it be safe to wrestle an untethered crocodile?
32. Do giraffes have more neck vertebrae than we do?
33. What makes a bird's back so stiff?
34. What is the connection between the bones on the top of your skull and corrugated cardboard?
35. If crocodiles had dentists, why would their bills be lower than ours?
36. Why are cracks in things like engine pylons so dangerous?
37. Why are most reptiles unable to keep warm at night, whereas most birds and mammals can?
38. What is stamina? How does the stamina of a crocodile compare with that of a lion?
39. Why do crocodiles become lifeless after extreme bouts of exercise?
40. What is the typical hunting strategy of a reptile? Why?
41. What are some of the advantages of being endothermic?
42. Give a major disadvantage of being endothermic.

43. Why do the peas on your plate cool down much faster than the baked potato?
44. What kind of animal was *Caudipteryx*?
45. Do you think *Archaeopteryx* could fly? Give two reasons for your answer.
46. Why do elephants cope better with the cold than with the heat?
47. How do mammals humidify and warm the air before it enters their lungs? Why is this so important?
48. What is keratin? Name two places where it is found.
49. What can an X ray of a dinosaur's nose tell us about its metabolic rate?
50. Give four features of *Tyrannosaurus* that show it was a carnivore.
51. What evidence is there that *Tyrannosaurus* fed upon other dinosaurs?
52. Why do hyenas eat bones?
53. Give some examples of sexual dimorphism.
54. Is it possible to tell the sex of a *Tyrannosaurus* skeleton?
55. What single feature of a horse's leg shows it is a faster runner than an elephant?
56. Why don't elephants gallop?
57. Give one reason why *Tyrannosaurus* may have avoided running fast.
58. What might have been the function of the small front limbs of *Tyrannosaurus*?
59. Give an example of allometry.
60. Do you think *Tyrannosaurus* was a scavenger, or an active predator?

Glossary

Air sac: A thin-walled sac that is part of the breathing apparatus of a bird and is interconnected with the lungs.

Abdominal cavity: The space lying immediately posterior to the diaphragm that houses the abdominal organs, like the liver, stomach, intestine.

Allometry: The phenomenon of different parts of the body growing at different rates during development. Our heads grow slower than our bodies, which is why babies have relatively large heads compared with their bodies.

Alveolar lungs: Lungs that have alveoli. Mammals have alveolar lungs.

Alveolus: A minute sac, the smallest subdivision of the lung of a mammal.

Alula: The small winglike projection from the leading edge of a bird's wing, the equivalent of the bird's thumb.

Ambient temperature: The surrounding temperature. This can be outdoors or indoors, depending on the location of the individual.

Anterior: Toward the front. Opposite to posterior.

Antorbital: In front of the orbit, as in the antorbital fenestra in the skull of *Tyrannosaurus* and other theropods.

Ascending process of the astragalus: A triangular extension from the proximal end of the astragalus, which overlaps the distal end of the tibia.

Astragalus: A bone in the ankle that articulates with the distal end of the tibia.

Barb: One of many side branches from the central midrib, or rachis, of a bird's feather.

Barbule: A small branch from the barb of a bird's feather.

Bipedal: Moving on two legs. We are bipedal; so are kangaroos and birds.

Capillary: The smallest of blood vessels. The walls of capillaries are only one cell thick.

Caudal vertebra: A vertebra of the tail.

Centrum: The main part, or body, of a vertebra. Adjacent vertebrae articulate together by their centra, which are held together by intervertebral discs.

Cervical: Pertaining to the neck, as in the cervical vertebrae.

Chevron: In reptiles, the Y-shaped bone that articulates with the posterior edge of the ventral surface of a caudal vertebra.

Clade: A group of organisms that share the same ancestor.

Cladistics: A method of classifying organisms based on the possession of shared derived (specialized) characters.

Clavicle: The collarbone.

Common ancestor: An ancestor shared by all the organisms in a particular group. All mammals, for example, share a common (unknown) ancestor.

Contour feather: The typical feather of a bird, with a rachis and stiff vane.

Convergent: Superficial similarities shared by animals, not because they are closely related, but because they do similar things. Whales, for example, look like fishes, not because they are closely related but because they too live in the sea and are similarly streamlined. Whales and fishes are said to be convergent.

Coracoid: The most proximal of the two bones forming the pectoral girdle. In reptiles, the coracoid tends to be discoidal.

Costal: Pertaining to the ribs.

Costal ventilation: Ventilation involving movements of the ribs.

Cursorial: Adapted for running. Cheetahs and gazelles are cursorial, as are cats and dogs, but elephants and mice are not cursorial.

Derived character: A specialized character that unites organisms believed to share a common ancestor. The possession of hair is a derived character shared by all mammals.

Diaphragm: A muscular partition that stretches across the base of the rib cage and is largely responsible for ventilating the lungs (breathing) in mammals.

Distal: Furthest from the body. The hand is distal to the forearm.

Dorsal: Toward the back, as opposed to ventral. Our vertebral column is dorsal to our sternum.

Dorsal vertebrae: Of reptiles, the vertebrae that lie between the pectoral girdle and sacrum. In birds and mammals these are referred to as thoracic and lumbar vertebrae.

Dromaeosaur: A group of theropod dinosaurs that includes *Velociraptor* and *Deinonychus*.

Ectothermic: Obtaining heat from outside the body, from the sun. Reptiles are ectothermic.

Endothermic: Generating heat from within the body. Mammals and birds are endothermic because of the high activity levels (metabolic rate) of their body cells.

Femur: The upper bone of the hind leg; the thighbone.

Fenestra: A perforation, as in the perforations in the side of the skull of *Tyrannosaurus*. Means *window* in Latin.

Fibula: The more slender of the two bones of the lower part of the hind leg. The fibula runs along the outside of the tibia (shinbone).

Forked sternal bone: The informal term used in the text for a forked bone in a developing bird that eventually fuses with the rest of the sternum.

Furcula: The wishbone. Found in most living birds and in some theropod dinosaurs.

Gait: A pattern of moving on land. The walk is a gait. So is the gallop.

Gallop: A gait characterized by a leaping movement, pushing off with the hind legs and landing on the front ones. During the leap, all four feet are off the ground at one point. Only quadrupeds can gallop.

Glycogen body: A structure of uncertain function found in the spinal region of living birds.

Gut: The alimentary canal, the organ of digestion, which commences at the back of the throat (the start of the esophagus) and continues to the end of the rectum.

Hadrosaur: Ornithischian dinosaurs, often referred to as duck-billed, because of the bill-like expansion of the snout and lower jaws. Common herbivores of the Cretaceous Period.

Hallux: The big toe. Also see *Reversed hallux*.

Head of the femur: The rounded process at the upper end of the femur that articulates with the hip socket.

Hepatic piston: The unique pistonlike liver of the crocodile, which functions to ventilate the lungs.

Heterocoelic: Adjective used to describe the saddle-shaped centra of birds.

Herbivorous: Plant-eating. Cows are herbivorous animals.

Homologous: Referring to similar structures that occur in animals sharing a common ancestor. A dolphin's front flipper is homologous with the front flipper of a seal and with the front limb of any other mammal, because all mammals share a common ancestor. But it is not homologous with the front fin of a shark.

Humerus: The upper bone of the foreleg.

Ilium: The most dorsal of the three bones forming the pelvic girdle. The ilium articulates with the sacrum.

Ischium: The most posterior of the two bones of the pelvic girdle that lie ventral to the ilium.

Keel of the sternum: The ventral sheet of bone to which the main flight muscles attach in flying birds.

Lateral: Toward the side of the body. Our arms are lateral to our ribs.

Ligament: The tough white sinew that connects one bone to another. Tendons are similar, but they attach muscles to bones.

Major metacarpal: The informal term used in the text for the largest of the two metacarpals of a bird. These two bones eventually fuse together as the skeleton matures, forming the terminal segment of the wing skeleton.

Mandibles: The lower jaws.

Medial: Toward the middle. Our ribs are medial to our arms.

Metabolic rate: The rate at which an animal consumes oxygen.

Metacarpal: Part of the forelimb skeleton, equivalent to the palm of the hand.

Metatarsal: Part of the hind limb skeleton, equivalent to the sole of the foot.

Maxilla: One of the bones of the skull that forms part of the upper jaw.

Maxillary fenestra: A perforation in the maxilla, as found in the skull of *Tyrannosaurus*.

Monophyletic: Of a group, sharing a common ancestor. Birds, for example, are said to be monophyletic because they are all believed to share a common (unknown) ancestor.

Nares: The nostrils.

Neural arch: That portion of the vertebra that forms the neural canal, through which the spinal cord passes.

Neural spine: The medial process that extends dorsally from the neural arch of a vertebra. The neural spines are especially prominent in the dorsal vertebrae.

Neural canal: The canal formed by the neural arch, for passage of the spinal cord.

Orbit: The eye socket.

Ornithischia: A major subdivision of the dinosaurs, characterized by a four-pronged pelvis. Ornithischian dinosaurs include the hadrosaurs, stegosaurs, horned dinosaurs, and ankylosaurs.

Ossified: Converted into bone.

Pectoral girdle: The shoulder girdle.

Pelvic girdle: The pelvis.

Pneumatic: With reference to skeletons, this pertains to bones that are air-filled, as in many of the bones in the skeleton of a modern bird.

Pneumatic foramen: An aperture leading into the air-filled space inside a pneumatic bone. The humerus of the chicken has a well-developed pneumatic foramen.

Posterior: Toward the back, as opposed to anterior. A dog's tail is posterior to its head.

Pubis: The most anterior of the two bones of the pelvic girdle that lie ventral to the ilium.

Quadrupedal: Moving on four legs. A horse is quadrupedal.

Rachis: The central supporting structure in the feather of a bird.

Radius: The innermost bone of the forearm. Lies at the root of the thumb and is medial to the other forearm bone, the ulna.

Respiratory: Pertaining to breathing. The lungs are part of the respiratory system.

Respiratory turbinates: The scroll-like structures found in the nasal passages of mammals and birds, which heat and humidify the air before it reaches the lungs. They are bony in mammals and are often called turbinal bones. The turbinates are cartilaginous in birds.

Reversed hallux: A big toe that points backward, as in theropod dinosaurs such as *Tyrannosaurus* and in birds.

Sacrum: A series of vertebrae that are fused together to form an anchorage for the pelvic girdle.

Saurischia: A major subdivision of the dinosaurs, characterized by a three-pronged pelvis. Comprises the theropods and sauropods.

Sauropod: One of the two groups of Saurischian dinosaurs.

Sauropods are characterized by their large bodies, solid, robust limb bones, relatively small skulls, long necks and tails, and dorsally placed nares. *Apatosaurus* is a sauropod.

Scapula: The most distal of the two bones forming the pectoral girdle. The scapula is bladelike, and is attached to the underlying ribs by muscles.

Septae: Shelflike structures.

Septate lungs: Lungs with internal shelves rather than sacs. Reptiles and birds have septate lungs.

Sexual dimorphism: Differences between the sexes, as in the antlers of male deer, the brilliant plumage of most male birds, the larger size of men compared with women.

Sister groups: Two branches of a clade that share a common ancestor.

Spinal cord: The large nerve cord that runs along the back from the brain to the end of the vertebral column. Part of the central nervous system.

Stamina: The ability to maintain high levels of physical activity for extended periods of time. Mammals and birds have more stamina than reptiles.

Sternal bone: An informal term used in the text for a spade-shaped bone in a developing bird. It eventually fuses with the rest of the sternum.

Sternal rib: The most ventral rib, which lies between the vertebral rib and the sternum.

Sternum: The median ventral bone, to which the rib cage attaches. The sternum is well developed in birds, especially those that fly.

Tendon: The tough white sinew that connects a muscle to a bone. Ligaments are similar, but they attach bones together.

Tetrapod: Having four limbs. Birds, like humans, are bipedal tetrapods.

Theropod: One of the two groups of Saurischian dinosaurs. Theropod features include: three fingers, all ending in claws; three long metatarsal bones, tightly pressed together, which are often fused; three main toes and a short "big toe," all ending in claws; a femur that is slightly bowed forward; a fibula that is closely pressed against the tibia.

Thoracic: Of birds and mammals, that part of the body that lies between the pectoral and sacral regions.

Thoracic cavity: The space enclosed by the rib cage and the diaphragm, housing the heart and lungs.

Tibia: The major bone of the lower hind leg—the shinbone.

Trachea: The tube that connects the lungs to the throat: the windpipe.

Transverse processes: The paired lateral processes that extend from the base of the neural arch, on either side of a thoracic or dorsal vertebra. They articulate with the ribs.

Trot: A gait in which there are never more than two feet on the ground. Except in the slow trot, there are moments when all feet are off the ground.

Turbinal bones: See *Respiratory turbinates*.

Turbinates: See *Respiratory turbinates*.

Ulna: The outermost bone of the forearm. Lies lateral to the other forearm bone, the radius.

Uncinate process: The bony projection from the posterior edge of a bird's rib. It overlaps with the rib behind it, adding to the rigidity of the rib cage.

Vane: Of a feather, the main body of the structure, comprising the rachis and its barbs and barbules.

Ventilation: Breathing movements, which cause the lungs to inflate and deflate.

Ventral: Toward the lower surface, as opposed to dorsal. Our sternum is ventral to our vertebral column.

Vertebral column: The backbone.

Vertebral rib: The "regular" rib. Articulates with a vertebra, dorsally, and a sternal rib, or the sternum, ventrally. Vertebral ribs are usually forked.

Zygapophyses: The paired processes extending from the anterior and posterior regions of the neural arch of a vertebra, which articulate with those of the adjacent vertebrae. The articular surface of each anterior zygapophysis faces upward and inward, while that of a posterior zygapophysis faces downward and outward.

Further Reading

Alexander, R. McN. 1985. Mechanics of posture and gait of some large dinosaurs. *Zoological Journal of the Linnean Society,* 83:1–25.

———. 1989. *Dynamics of dinosaurs and other extinct giants.* New York, Columbia University Press.

Altagerel, P., M. A. Norell, L. M. Chiappe, and J. M. Clark. 1993. Flightless bird from the Cretaceous of Mongolia. *Nature,* 362:623–26.

Bakker, R. T. 1972. Anatomical and ecological evidence of endothermy in dinosaurs. *Nature,* 238:81–85.

———. 1980. Dinosaur heresy—dinosaur renaissance: Why we need endothermic archosaurs for a comprehensive theory of bioenergetic evolution. In *A cold look at the warm-blooded dinosaurs,* ed. R. D. K. Thomas and E. C. Olsen. Boulder: Westview Press.

———. 1986. *The dinosaur heresies.* New York: William Morrow and Co.

———, M. Williams, and P. Currie. 1988. *Nanotyrannus,* a new genus of pygmy tyrannosaur, from the latest Cretaceous of Montana. *Hunteria,* 1:1–30.

Bennett, A. F., R. S. Seymour, D. F. Bradford, and G. J. W. Webb. 1985. Mass-dependence of anaerobic metabolism and acid-base disturbances during activity in salt-water crocodile, *Crocodylus porosus. Journal of Experimental Biology,* 118:161–71.

Britt, B. B. 1997. Postcranial pneumaticity. In *Encyclopedia of Dinosaurs,* ed. P. J. Currie and K. Padian. New York: Academic Press.

Bryant, H. N. and A. P. Russell. 1993. The occurrence of clavicles within the Dinosauria: Implications for the homology of the avian furcula and the utility of negative evidence. *Journal of Vertebrate Paleontology,* 13:171–84.

Burke, A. C., and A. Feduccia. 1997. Developmental patterns and the identification of homologies in the avian hand. *Science,* 278:666–68.

Carpenter, K. 1990. Variation in *Tyrannosaurus rex*. In *Dinosaur Systematics: Approaches and Perspectives*, ed. K. Carpenter and P. J. Currie. Cambridge: Cambridge University Press. 140–45.

Chen, P.-J., Z. Dong, and S. Zhen. 1998. An exceptionally well-preserved theropod dinosaur from the Yixian Formation of China. *Nature,* 391:147–52.

Colbert, E. H. 1962. The weights of dinosaurs. *American Museum Novitates,* 2076:1–16.

Dal Sasso, C., and M. Signore. 1998. Exceptional soft-tissue preservation in a theropod dinosaur from Italy. *Nature,* 392:383–87.

Erickson, G. M., and K. H. Olson. 1996. Bite marks attributable to *Tyrannosaurus rex:* Preliminary description and implications. *Journal of Vertebrate Paleontology,* 16:175–78.

———, S. D. Van Kirk, J. Su., M. E. Levenston, W. E. Caler, and D. R. Carter. 1996. Bite-force estimation for *Tyrannosaurus rex* from tooth-marked bones. *Nature,* 382:705–08.

Farlow, J. O., M. B. Smith, and J. M. Robinson. 1995. Body mass, bone "strength indicator," and cursorial potential of *Tyrannosaurus rex*. *Journal of Vertebrate Paleontology*, 15:713–25.

Feduccia, A. 1996. *The Origin and Evolution of Birds*. New Haven: Yale University Press.

Forster, C. A., S. D. Sampson, L. M. Chiappe, and D. W. Krause. 1998. The theropod ancestry of birds: New evidence from the Late Cretaceous of Madagascar. *Science,* 279:1915–19.

Garner, J. P., and A. L. R. Thomas. 1998. In Counting the fingers of birds and dinosaurs, Chatterjee et al., *Science* Online, 280 (5362):355.

Hecht, M. K., J. H. Ostrom, G. Viohl, and P. Wellnhofer. 1985. *The Beginnings of Birds*. Freunde des Jura-Museums Eichstätt, Eichstätt, Germany.

Hinchliffe, R. 1997. The forward march of the bird-dinosaur halted? *Science,* 278:596–97.

Mackay, R. S. 1964. Galápagos tortoise and marine iguana deep body temperatures measured by radio telemetry. *Nature,* 204:355–58.

Makovicky, P. J., and P. J. Currie. 1998. The presence of the furcula in tyrannosaurid theropods, and its phylogenetic and functional implications. *Journal of Vertebrate Paleontology,* 18:143–49.

McGowan, C. 1989. Feather structure in flightless birds and its bearing on the question of the origin of feathers. *Journal of Zoology, London,* 218:537–47.

———. 1991. *Dinosaurs, spitfires, and sea dragons*. Cambridge, Mass.: Harvard University Press.

———. 1997. *The raptor and the lamb: Predators and prey in the living world.* New York: Henry Holt.

Padian, K. 1998. When is a bird not a bird? *Nature,* 393:729–30.

———, and L. M. Chiappe. 1998. The origin of birds and their flight. *Scientific American,* 2:39–47.

———, and L. M. Chiappe. 1998. The origin and early evolution of birds. *Biological Reviews,* 78:1–42.

Paul, G. S. 1988. Predatory dinosaurs of the world: A complete illustrated guide. New York: Simon and Schuster.

Perry, S. F. 1989. Mainstreams in the evolution of vertebrate respiratory structures. In *Form and function in birds,* ed. A. S. King and J. McLelland. London: Academic Press. 1–67.

Pooley, A. C., and C. Gans. 1976. The Nile crocodile. *Scientific American,* 234:114–24.

Qiang, J., P. J. Currie, M. A. Norell, and S.-A. Ji. 1998. Two feathered dinosaurs from northeastern China. *Nature,* 393:753–61.

Raath, M. A. 1990. Morphological variation in small theropods and its meaning in systematics: evidence from *Syntarsus rhodesiensis.* In *Dinosaur Systematics: Approaches and Perspectives,* ed. K. Carpenter and P. J. Currie. Cambridge: Cambridge University Press. 91–105.

Ruben, J. A., W. J. Hillenius, N. R. Geist, A. Leitch, T. D. Jones, P. J. Currie, J. R. Horner, and G. Espe III. 1996. The metabolic status of some Late Cretaceous Dinosaurs. *Science,* 273:1204–07.

———, T. D. Jones, N. R. Geist, and W. J. Hillenius. 1997. Lung structure and ventilation in theropod dinosaurs and early birds. *Science,* 278:1267–70.

Schmidt-Nielsen, K. 1971. How birds breathe. *Scientific American,* 225: 73–79.

Sereno, P. C., and F. E. Novas. 1992. The complete skull and skeleton of an early dinosaur. *Science,* 258:1137–40.

———, C. A. Forster, R. R. Rogers, and A. M. Monetta. 1993. Primitive dinosaur skeleton from Argentina and the early evolution of Dinosauria. *Nature,* 361:64–66.

Solounias, N. 1997. Remarkable findings regarding the evolution of the giraffe neck. *Journal of Vertebrate Paleontology,* 17 (supplement to no. 3): 78A.

Unwin, D. M. 1998. Feathers, filaments and theropod dinosaurs. *Science,* 391:119–20.

Wellnhofer, P. 1988. A new specimen of *Archaeopteryx. Science,* 240:1790–92.

Skull Cutouts

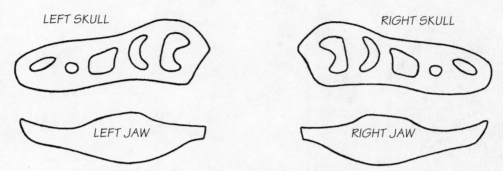

LEFT SKULL

RIGHT SKULL

LEFT JAW

RIGHT JAW

Cutouts for the skull and lower jaw.

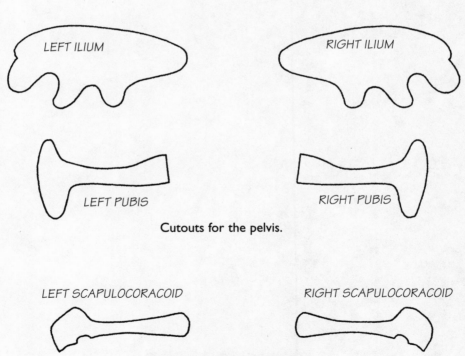

LEFT ILIUM

RIGHT ILIUM

LEFT PUBIS

RIGHT PUBIS

Cutouts for the pelvis.

LEFT SCAPULOCORACOID

RIGHT SCAPULOCORACOID

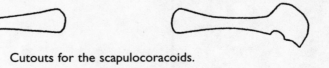

Cutouts for the scapulocoracoids.

The Talented T. Rex Builders: From Chicken Bones to *T. Rex*

...And Among Their *Apatosauri*...

Praise for *T. Rex to Go* and *Make Your Own Dinosaur out of Chicken Bones*

▼▼▼ "Building a dinosaur from chicken bones was challenging, exciting, engaging to all—and fun. I can think of no better hands-on anatomy project."

> —Judith Miller Smith
> teacher, Jefferson County Open School
> Lakewood, Colorado

▼▼▼ "Lots of fun! A real sense of accomplishment when you finish. This project is for someone who is sick of building plastic models, likes dinosaurs, and loves chicken!"

> —A. J. Devaux (age 12)

▼▼▼ "Chris McGowan's two books represent the best money I've ever spent. They kept A.J. fascinated over two summers, as well as providing the answer to that eons-old question, 'What's for supper?' "

> —Deb Devaux, A.J.'s stepmom

▼▼▼ "Not only did I have a great time constructing the *T. rex* out of chicken bones, I also learned a lot about the skeletal features of the large theropod dinosaurs and your average chicken!"

> —Katie Hoffman (age 14)

▼▼▼ "My kids (Alexa, 3½, and Rachel, 5½) loved helping with the dinosaur. From finishing their chicken dinners ('Here's another bone for the dinosaur, Daddy') to cleaning and sorting the bones, they had a good time. They occasionally remember the names of their leg bones ('Is this my femur?') and have seen how muscles attach to bones and how they work together. . . . An excellent book! One I'm recommending highly to others."

> —Stephen M. Platt, Ph.D.,
> software engineer

Index